CH00644570

Garden Cities of To-morrow

A manifesto

Yves Cabannes & Philip Ross
New Garden City Movement
Share, enjoy, prosper

**21ˢᵗ Century Garden Cities
of To-morrow. A manifesto**

by Yves Cabannes & Philip Ross

Copyright ©
Yves Cabannes, Philip Ross 2012, 2013.
All rights reserved.
ISBN 978-1-291-47827-3

First edition, May 2013

Word diagrams produced by wordle.net.

All reasonable efforts have been made by the authors to
contact the copyright holders of work reproduced in this
volume. The authors will be pleased to make good any
omissions or rectify any mistakes brought to their attention at
the earliest opportunity.

www.newgardencitymovement.org.uk
Yves Cabannes - ycabanes@mac.com
Philip Ross - rosspe@talk21.com

Published at: www.Lulu.com
20 May 2014

Prof. Yves Cabannes

Professor Yves Cabannes is an Urban Planner and activist specialising in urban and municipal development, with particular interest in urban agriculture & Food sovereignty, local currencies, participatory planning, municipal public policies, low cost housing, participatory budgeting, community-based micro credit systems and appropriate technologies for local development. From 2007 on, he is Professor and Chair of Development Planning at Bartlett Development Planning Unit (DPU), University College London and was previously lecturer at Harvard University Graduate School of Design. From 1997 to 2004, he was the regional Coordinator of the UN Habitat/UNDP Urban Management Program for Latin America and the Caribbean.

He is currently member of the board of the International RUAF Foundation - Resource Centres for Urban Agriculture and Food Security-, The World Fund for City Development (Metropolis), *HuiZhi* (Participation Centre, Chengdu, China) and the Participatory Budgeting Project (USA).

Philip Ross

Philip Ross was Mayor of Letchworth Garden City from 2007-9 and an outspoken advocate and defender of Garden City values and principles. In 2009, he won a landmark High Court battle that ensured that the Letchworth Heritage Foundation - who managed the garden city estate - remained accountable to the people of the town. He has spoken and written on the issue of Garden Cities and sustainable development in both the UK and China. He is a Chartered Engineer and has worked as an IT and business specialist at many leading software companies and major banks in the UK. He served for seven years as a trustee of the British Computer Society. He currently works in London for a small specialist business consultancy.

Acknowledgements

We would like to thank those who have inspired us to write this.

Contents

Boxes

Foreword \ Forward!

I enthusiastically agreed to writing this forward as I travelled from the University of Jordan in Amman, where one of the professors, Dr Kamel Mahadin, said there is a single rule for cities –"Plant as many trees as you can", to Tsinghua University in Beijing where an equally famous professor, Wu Liangyong said "gardens bring happiness to people."

The two authors complement each other beautifully, one a visionary and gutsy politician, the other a gifted academic with a deep routed social conscience. With the benefit of a century of post Letchworth Garden City knowledge and the lessons of two World Wars, their timely released book re-brands the garden city from a social as well as a technical point of view. It says it's a manifesto for 21st Century Garden Cities of Tomorrow, but it could equally be a manifesto for decent human urban survival on our cherished Planet.

It concentrates on the role of each citizen - his or her responsibilities and opportunities. It advocates restoring basic human values back to ordinary people, away from the, "I'm doing you a favour" private pro-bono benefaction and/or cash-starved governmental institutions that seem to know the cost of everything, but the value of nothing.

It explains participatory budgeting – what's that? It's where ordinary residents have the power to democratically allocate money, identify and prioritise local expenditure, and monitor results. In Brazil, with 25 years of experience of participatory budgeting, even the favelas (slums) are benefitting.

No need to demolish these slums any more, the slum dwellers have a say in what happens to their communities. Prior to participatory budgeting, local authorities could only come up with wholesale demolition of slum communities, a bit like Britain after the 2nd World War up until the 1969 Housing Act.

Manchester City Council's Public Health Inspector, Alf Young, was credited with destroying more houses than the Luftwaffe, because in his Orwellian vision they were 'unfit for human habitation.' His mass demolition policies left Manchester with acres of cleared land made available for mass-redevelopment and Mancunians got modern places like Hulme!

Readers, don't bother trying to find re-developed Hulme. Like other brave new world deck-access concrete estates, modern Hulme is no more, it suffered the same fate as the Victorian terraces that were destroyed to make way for it . What a waste of money, time and the shattered lives of confused Manchester folk.

Out of this pathetic failure, there is a silver lining! Yes, whether in Brazil or Britain, sustainability, as we know it today, was born out of the debris/hardcore and the un-sustainable waste of the Modern Movement. Are we there yet? I said are we there yet? No. Only 2 billion slum dwellers (UN Habitat projected 2030 figures) left to sort out.

Yes, these two distinguished authors are concerned about saving our Planet, not in a pompous, self-important, un-readable style, but down to earth and rooted into the British garden city movement – so it is real! Most pioneering initiatives are by implication ahead of their time. The successful garden city movement is no different.

This book will help launch a Renaissance of appreciation for something we got right. It has taken 100 years or so for us to see how forward thinking Ebenezer Howard, the man who brought us Letchworth, must have been. This handy little number can be read in one go and it will make you proud that the British garden city movement got it right, and the rest of the world followed. Sustainability all the way!

Chris Maser, another writer on sustainable community development, said, "A sense of community often begins in a garden." He was right

– he also saw the Ebenezer Howard initiative encouraging nature into urban design as a positive, compared with most of 19th century Industrial Revolution housing - Saltaire excepted. Different, but not just militarily inspired, Baron Haussmann, in 19th century Paris, could also be considered a nature lover with what became wide tree-lined avenues, and Jaime Lerner, (another mayor and an architect - all in one person – authors note) with his 'green fingers', bringing the Parana forest into the heart of the city of Curitiba.

There is only one thoroughfare in Letchworth, Cross Street, the rest is a garden, and what a garden. No self-respecting urban planner or architect dares to ignore Ebenezer Howard's wish to create a sustainable green Utopia, Freiburg, Chengdu, Masdar (not a garden city – yet!), Singapore comes to mind.

There is an important message in this book, it's healthy to have flowers and trees in our cities, without them, mankind will die; the microclimate brings residents' well-being, better mental and physical health which improves their quality of life. Residents' self-help, proximity with nature, "breathe the air" – oh I feel better already, "I grew the vegetables in my own garden", ordinary people participating in ecological things, echoes of "Dig for Victory" - but this time in peacetime!

As more and more agricultural land is being used for building, existing cities offer replacement land for urban agriculture in streets, squares, building roofs, walls and balconies. Check out downtown Havana! It's not just a UNESCO World Heritage Site, but also a WUAGS – A World Urban Agricultural Site – yes you read it here first, but feel free to use the new acronym! As the wise Chengdu resident said, "Ruralising the town – not urbanising the countryside."

Greenery reduces air temperature. Trees are great in dealing with oxygen/Co2 magic, drainage and water run-off while preserving scarce water, especially in desert regions. It lets the wind blow, the sun shine and enough moisture to let things grow.

That's the technical bit, but the book bravely gets involved with politics and social things. Mrs Thatcher is quoted – no, not "there's no such thing as society", but a more reflective reference. Lenin gets a mention, Marxism, the French and Russian Revolutions, the Paris commune, Stalingrad, fairness, social justice stuff, co-operatives, a manifesto for zero waste and zero carbon urban environments.

I love the bit on happiness. No mention of Bhutan, but the wealth and harmony of a Garden City are measured through the happiness of its citizens.

Yeah, well, Philip Ross (which University will be the first to offer you an honorary doctorate?) and Yves Cabannes (who has come a long way since Harvard, but has not become the Mayor of London yet!), a good book is measured by the happiness it brings to its readers. I, for one, am happy – thank you.

The book introduces the general reader to Wordle™, those wonderful word clouds that reflect, size wise, the number of references to the most used words in a chapter or section of the book – try it (available free on Google) when you next write a love letter! Until then have a good solid read. Share, enjoy, prosper - yeah!

Dr Rod Hackney
October 2013

Dr Rod Hackney, director of Kansara Hackney Ltd, Past President of the Royal Institute of British Architects (PPRIBA), Past President of the International Union of Architects (PPUIA), "pioneering father of Barefoot Community Architecture". www.kansarahackney.com

How to become a Garden City

Over 100 years ago, Ebenezer Howard set out on an intellectual journey to define what would make a Garden City. The result, in 1898, was his book 'Garden Cities of Tomorrow – the peaceful path to reform'. It was written in an age where the memory of the Paris Commune was still fresh, where Marxism was still being formulated, where imperial Europe was at its zenith and a young Lenin was still in a reflective mood.

The book led to the founding of Letchworth Garden City, the world's first Garden City. Not though as an architectural project - it didn't set out to build chocolate box houses in some sort of faux utopia but instead it aimed to build a new sort of town and community. Great things are built from dreams. In this world, the citizen would be King and the ills of the time – landlords, squalor, pollution and poverty -

would be tackled and beaten. Howard had been reflecting on the industrialisation process that was still underway in Britain at the time. He aimed to bring the best of town and country together in the ideal town. Printed word attempted to become reality when funding was found to purchase an estate of land and build this new town. This town would not be built out of benevolence, paternalism or charity or as a 'good work', as was the case with towns like Port Sunlight and Bournville, but would be built because it was just and fair for the people that would live there. At its heart was the radical proposition of the common ownership of land as its key foundation. A young Lenin visited the town and was influenced by the ideas. He stayed there as a guest of religious minister, Bruce Wallace, the man who rented his Brotherhood Church in London to the fifth congress of the Russian Social Democratic Labour Party (RSDLP). If you visit Letchworth today you will see the Brotherhood Hall in the town near the cinema. Indeed the early Bolsheviks were Garden City enthusiasts.

When Letchworth was built new inspiring architecture was a key component and the layout of the town was planned with simple rules that reflected common sense and the common wealth- so factories were placed in the east so the smoke didn't blow over the town. The architects were inspired by the arts and crafts movement[1] and driven by a belief in green spaces, a healthy environment and a sympathetic layout. These were the watchwords to guide this new utopia. However, Howard and his supporters knew that there was more to a good community and a town than just sympathetic architecture; the social aspects would be of key importance with ownership and citizenship as key ingredients. In a way they were not town planners but community architects.

Socialist architects Parker and Unwin were soon helping to design Hampstead Garden suburb and other areas. Parker travelled to Brazil and to North America. New towns and cities throughout the world would be and continue to be inspired by the book and the ideas. In the UK in the 1920's Welwyn Garden City was built on a grander scale than that of Letchworth by Louis de Soissons and Kenyon.

Sadly, it was the architecture and designs principles that would be copied and celebrated as architects tried again and again to build the perfect city or town through bricks and mortar alone. Garden Cities became the acceptable face of town and city planning.

Perhaps the great example of this is Stalingrad, built in 1928 by Semyonov (who had been in exile in Letchworth) and his colleagues, largely on Garden City principles. City ownership of land, however, with its democratically controlled revenue based on co-operative principles, was excluded as the centralist command structure became operative throughout Soviet society.

When Welwyn Garden City was built the project was adopted by the Government and the community ownership aspects were relegated to the back of the scheme - though a number of co-operative type projects remained. The 1917 revolution in Russia with its emphasis on common ownership had its effect. The need for housing was accepted - 'homes for heroes' - but the dangerous policy of collective local ownership was not.

Just as the Soviets lost their way, Letchworth followed suit. Once it had been hated by the Daily Mail (a UK newspaper) for its radical population and its radical views. The pioneers of the movement and the Daily Worker saw that as a cause for celebration. By the 1950's though, the Daily Worker had long since been replaced by the Daily Mail and the town returned a Conservative MP. It dropped the suffix 'Garden City' as it no longer wanted to be associated with that radical past. Ironically, in 2003 it was restored as it now sounded sufficiently twee and helped the value of house prices. By then Garden City was associated, even in Letchworth, with gardens and flowers, not radical politics or dangerous ideas. Since then Letchworth has had its fair share of debate, change and discussion and argument about what it stands for and where it is going.

Today Ebenezer's old company still exists in the town but has gone from being a private company to being a public corporation in 1962, and then 33 years later in

1995, it became a private company again, but with declared charitable objectives. During its journey through these different governance models and with different leaders the company had evolved and changed, sometimes for the better and sometimes for the worse. Now in 2013 it has a clearer direction and a better understanding of its accountability to the town and the people within it. Given that it is now more than 110 years since the founding of the first Garden City, with all this subsequent history and experience of town design, community development and application of the Garden City model, we ask what lessons can be learned. What should the principles of a 21st century Garden City be? We believe many of Howard's original instincts to be correct, but how can these be delivered in a modern setting? Not forgetting too that while Europe has largely completed its process of industrialisation China, Africa, South America and many other places it is still very much a current concern.

This book aims to define and justify the principles that should underpin a Garden City in the 21st century. The ideas in this book come as a result of a meeting of minds and ideas sparked at a meeting of the China-Europa Forum in Wuhan and Hong Kong and in speaking and discussing issues with delegates from Lisbon, Colombia, Wuhan, Chengdu, Hong Kong, Amsterdam, London and subsequently meeting and speaking with people from Cuba, Ecuador and Venezuela.

It is not a one size fits all approach, not all components can be present. We note too that it is not just new towns that can be a Garden City, any town and every town should aspire to it. This pamphlet describes and defines the principles and values that should be believed and acted upon and explains why we think that they are important.

What makes a
21st Century Garden City?

A Garden City is a fair, just and harmonious community. It is not restricted to new cities or towns or those built following traditional Garden City town planning, architectural or design principles. A Garden City is about community not merely about architecture and urban design.

It is about building a harmonious community, balancing the best of town and country together to a community where the measure of success is ultimately the happiness of the people who live in it. Below are listed twelve principles that we believe underline a Garden City. Some are methods and others are objectives. In effect these principles represent doorways into the Garden City, you can enter using one of the many doorways but contradict or deny any of the principles then they will also prove themselves to be exits. We declare that any town, city or neighbourhood can be considered as a Garden City if it embraces the following principles:

1. *Residents are Citizens.*

2. *The Garden City owns itself.*

3. *The Garden City is energy efficient and carbon neutral.*

4. *Provides access to land for living and working to all.*

5. *Fair Trade principles are practised.*

6. *Prosperity is shared.*

7. *All citizens are equal, all citizens are different.*

8. *There is fair representation and direct democracy.*

9. *Garden Cities are produced through participatory planning and design methods.*

10. *A City of Rights that builds and defends the Right to the City*

11. *Knowledge is held in common, shared and enhanced.*

12. *Wealth and harmony measured by happiness.*

1. Residents are Citizens

Residents consider themselves to be citizens of the Garden City. This includes people who also work, participate and use the Garden City. They are aware that the town truly belongs to them. There is a culture of rights, duties and responsibilities that comes through citizenship. The town is run for the common good, reflecting and representing the common will with a belief in equality and fraternity as the city is run for the benefit of the many, not the few.

2. The Garden City owns itself

The Garden City is ultimately owned by its local community and not by a series of landlords. This ownership and governance is derived from the people who live and work in the city and who are its citizens acting for the common good. If the Garden City is its own landlord then it is answerable to and controlled by its citizens, ideally as a Community Land Trust managed by democratic structures that make it both inclusive and accountable.

3. The Garden City is energy efficient and carbon neutral

A Garden City has a harmonious relationship with nature and is energy efficient. A Garden City is a carbon neutral city and does not pollute. It's planning, design and resources are deployed to achieve this goal. Citizens and the Government in the Garden City have a collective responsibility in their daily lives to design and implement such policies. This could be ensuring the provision of clean, safe and efficient public transport, the ability to navigate the Garden City by walking or cycling on one hand and the ability to reduce waste, recycle and reuse resources by citizens on the other.

4. Provide access to land for living and working to all

The Garden City promotes urban agriculture, the ability for citizens to grow most of their own food, even in an urban area. There is a right of free and fair access to the land for all residents to grow their own food whether it is through common allotments, common land, farms, productive streets and parks or private gardens. Alongside this is the right to affordable housing and also the right of access to resources in urban areas to build or run their individual or collective businesses or workshops.

It is a productive city that aims at its own self-sufficiency providing opportunities for agricultural work, crafts, commerce and industry. Rents are provided to encourage self-sufficiency and regeneration, provided in partnership with tenants, not just for tenants. The goal is for the City to be productive and sustainable in its own right, not as a dormitory settlement or a place of mere consumption.

5. Fair Trade principles are practised

The Garden City is committed to the practises and ethics of Fair Trade implementing the credo that it's prosperity is not built upon the suffering of others, whether inside its own city limits, inside its own country or internationally.

6. Prosperity is shared

The prosperity of the Garden City is shared in practise among all its citizens, not just among the rich, wealthy and establishment. Participatory budgeting through which citizens decide on the priorities for public and community investment is one of the key mechanisms in practise. To secure the wealth and trigger jobs among the community it can create local or a complementary community currency and set up community banks.

7. All citizens are equal, all citizens are different

All citizens in a Garden City are equal regardless of how long they have lived there or how many generations of their family have. There are no special privileges for anyone. A Garden City provides support, treats with dignity those with mental and physical disabilities and values each citizen, irrespective of their religious or sexual orientation.

8. Fair representation and direct democracy

There is a right to participate in the Garden City, in what the city does, how it is run and who does what. A Garden City can be made up of many cities and towns but each of these will be comprised of different neighbourhoods and communities, each with differing needs and aspirations. The prosperity of the Garden City is employed to help those in greatest need. Each community and neighbourhood should be empowered and encouraged to form its own free and open association, council or forum to represent and engage the views and needs of that local community. The Garden City will share its decision making. It will devolve some to representatives but by also by engaging directly and meaningfully with the citizens so all can have an informed say and collective decision making power on the priorities for the Garden City.

9. Garden Cities are produced through participatory planning and design methods

A Garden City is in harmony with the landscape, water, air, nature and the surrounding countryside. New developments and housing have Garden City space and design characteristics and aim to promote the health and wellbeing of its citizens, current and future and are developed through participatory methods on fundamental issues, not just cosmetic ones. Public spaces are widely available as an important concept as it provides the means for people to meet and share views and to integrate. These public spaces and facilities bring together young and old, rich and poor, those of different races, religions and backgrounds as a community that celebrates and rejoices in its diversity and exercises tolerance and freedom.

10. *A City of Rights that builds and defends the Right to the City*

In the Garden City there are universal rights for all citizens such as the right to clean air, the right to nutritious food, the right to adequate housing, the right to work and fair wages. There are not only individual rights but collective rights such as the collective right to enjoy the city and its majesty as well as collective civic and political rights. In traditional terms, as the City is held in common there is a collective right to these commons. The Right to the City is a superior Right as it is both individual and collective.

11. *Knowledge is held in common, shared and enhanced*

A Garden City is a mutual city that builds a culture of production, sharing and co-operation, not just in terms of its prosperity and governance but also in terms of the knowledge it acquires and generates. It shares and co-operates for the good of the City while still operating competition to create innovation and development.

12. *Wealth and harmony measured by happiness*

The wealth and harmony of the Garden City is measured in the happiness its citizens. It is the only true measurement of a successful city. Their happiness is not based upon the suffering or expense of others.

These are the characteristics of a Garden City, not all can be present but the guiding principles of a new Garden City will be to: Share, Enjoy and Prosper.

What turns the sharing of the Garden City's prosperity from an act of paternalism or charity to one of empowerment and citizenship? It is people not just having a share in the City's prosperity but a share – an active say – in how it is spent and what and where it is spent on. It means people having a chance to participate and speak for themselves and make informed decisions.

[1] Residents are Citizens

Residents consider themselves citizens of the Garden City. This includes people who also work, participate and use the Garden City. They are aware that the town truly belongs to them. There is a culture of rights, duties and responsibilities that comes through citizenship. The town is run for the common good, reflecting and representing the common will with a belief in equality and fraternity as the city is run for the benefit of the many, not the few.

A Garden City belongs to the people that live in it, who work in it and those who participate in it - they are its citizens. They will own and participate in the Garden City and will support its principles. We believe that the special ingredient that turns bricks and mortar, steel and concrete from simply being houses, factories and offices into a community is *citizenship*. This comes through active participation and participation.

The goal of a Garden City is therefore to create a city or town full of citizens. A Garden City should be almost like a city-state - there is a sense of belonging, purpose and pride from living and working there. This is derived from a sense of ownership, participation and belief in the Garden City principles.

Citizenship does extend to those working in the City whether they are commuters from outside or migrant workers from hundreds or thousands of miles away. Citizenship is based on individuals; it is not based on capital stakes, though the Garden City will support and recognise the contribution of its capital investors, but is a City where people come first.

Without this sense of citizenship there is no Garden City because a Garden City isn't bricks and mortar but it is a state of mind. Perhaps it is a bit like being in love; no one can tell you that you are you just know it.

The question is how to achieve this sense of being and also how to scale up such a sense of belonging from the smallest village of a few hundred to a city of many millions.

The simplest of answers is that it has to be driven by principles that everyone can embrace.

The twelve defined principles in this text are all important but in a Garden City context none of them can stand alone. This is especially true for the concept of citizenship. It is the product of the other principles coming together to form a successful Garden City. Without citizenship you have Garden City in name only and the converse is true that without citizenship the other principles won't work. They are mutually dependent on each other.

The City will be used by many different groups such as individuals, families, co-operatives, other voluntary groups as well as commercial and industrial groups.

We propose the common ownership of the city through a community land trust or similar, but this form of ownership can only be effective if it is accountable because only by being accountable can it share its prosperity fairly. Yet this accountability only works if residents are empowered enough to realise that individually and collectively they have the power to question, scrutinise and hold to account those operating the Garden City. (See box 1 on the rebirth of citizenship in France and boxes 2 and 3 for British values). By doing so they become citizens but in doing so they have to be citizens and share the dividends and gain the benefits of it.

This suggests that Citizenship is very much a state of mind, but a very important one. So while citizenship remains as a principle it is also an objective and a practice.

The allegory you could draw is that citizenship is the level of fitness that the city needs to achieve to become a Garden City and the other principles are the exercises that the city needs to undertake to achieve this level of fitness.

Box 1. Rebirth of Citizenship

Members of the third estate began the French Revolution in June 1789 by swearing an oath not to separate until a constitution had been written for France - the 'Serment du jeu de paume'. The French Revolution saw the rebirth of the concept of citizenship after which people referred to each other as 'citoyen'.

Entitlement and empowerment

Citizenship isn't about entitlement, it is about empowerment. It is not run by the state but by the people who live and work in it for themselves. It is a very empowering city. It is not about taxing the rich to give to the poor or taking from one group to give to another, it is about sharing the city together and sharing its prosperity. The prosperity doesn't have to be taxed from the rich because technically speaking it is retained within the city and within common ownership. It is not about taxing prosperity or success but about sharing it. Just as we share the air we breathe.

Box 2. British Entitlement and Rights

In Britain one of the biggest challenges facing 21st century governments is welfare reform. Post war governments delivered welfare reforms and support to help the poorest and those in most need, but they failed to deliver a sense of citizenship. During the second World War the nation did come together but that spirit is now lost. Britain struggles with a large welfare budget and a culture of entitlement but is there one of citizenship? The old British model of charity and paternalism has persisted. We have subjects demanding entitlements and relying on charity and paternalism. It is interesting that William Beveridge's original challenge for the British welfare state was that citizens should be enabled to take "private action for social advance[2]."

If we had to define citizenship then we would say that entitlement only comes through empowerment. It is as much about liberty, being given the freedom, ability and resources to choose to solve your own problems. An entrepreneurial creed should be strong in the Garden City as people and the community think about how to generate their share, not how to get their share. The fact is that it is about both individual and collective empowerment. It supersedes and goes beyond political divides.

Box 3. Solidarity, tennis and equality

Garden Cities are a place of solidarity and refuge. One interesting story is that Britain's most famous tennis player Fred Perry was brought up at Brentham Garden Suburb near Ealing, London. His father was the national secretary of the national Co-operative Party and when they moved to London a place was found for him in the Garden Suburb. The supply of tennis courts and facilities in tune with Garden City values delivered a tennis champion for Britain. But his background didn't go down well with the class-conscious nature of the Lawn Tennis Club of Great Britain and in 1934 after beating Australia's Jack Crawford to win his first Wimbledon title he was due to receive the striped tie to signify his automatic membership of the All England Club. This was traditionally presented with some ceremony but Perry's was simply left draped over his clothes in the changing-room.

Citizenship with a sense of worth: becoming a citizen

How can this sense of worth be created? Citizenship can't be given, it has to be earned or in a historical sense, taken. In Milton Parc, Montreal, Canada, Vermont, USA and Burlington,[3] applicants who wish to join their community land trust (CLT) or housing co-operative are required to undergo training or an induction process so that they fully understand what they are joining and what they will be part of. The success of the CLTs and their lack of foreclosures during the economic crisis are partly attributed to this training and induction process which meant that people took informed decisions.

In some organisations when someone becomes a member of the group they read out the charter to the other members and become legitimised in the eyes of their new group. This is true of the co-ops in France known as the Sociétés Ouvrière Coopérative de Production (SCOP). Induction ceremonies can successfully reinforce the values of organization. In the UK there are citizenship courses for people who wish to become British citizens. Aspiring citizens have to learn about some British history, national organisation and other cultural traditions following which there is a Citizenship Ceremony.

Incentives for citizenship

The immediate question for Garden Cities is why should people have to do this just to live there? The answer is that they don't have to (as the co-op principles state membership should be voluntary), but if they want to become an active citizen in the town then they would be encouraged to.

Box 4. Letchworth Garden City - The echo of citizenship?

When I [Philip] moved to Letchworth Garden City in 2000 - although much of the Garden City movement has vanished - echoes remained of its past in the language that people used. I read in old books that people talked of being *'citizens of Letchworth Garden City',* I found that the term still had resonance – a slight tiny echo of a hidden radical past. People could refer to themselves as a citizen of Letchworth Garden City but would not say that they were a citizen of Tunbridge Wells or of Luton. Why is this? Where has it come from? The only explanation is in the very roots of the town itself. Ebenezer Howard, on founding the town said that it should belong to the people that live there that they would be their own landlord. That doesn't mean that people feel that they are, but feel that they should be.

One way to encourage this would be that if the Garden City dispensed dividends from its prosperity then the issue of these would be limited to those residents registered as citizens, but by undertaking training or an induction, it offers other values. For new people arriving in the city it provides the chance for them to meet other people and to integrate.

Feeling like a Citizen

You can't just tell people that they are Citizens; they must choose to become citizens and be empowered to do so. It is like a worker who chooses to become a shareholder in the company he works for. He subtly changes the relationship with the firm, in both circumstances he is a stakeholder in the firm as both an employee and then as a shareholder. Just as becoming a shareholder in a company is something you choose to do, the same must be true of becoming a citizen. It must be something that people actively choose to do because it must be an empowering act and not an act of paternalism. Box 4 explains how in Letchworth people felt like 'citizens'.

Citizenship - What should happen in practice

The Garden City citizen should share the ethics and values of the City and they develop and exercise their citizenship by supporting and defending the implementation of those values, which are in effect the other principles discussed herein.

- Community Land Trust: means that citizen now has a tangible stake in the City and is in effect a shareholder in it. Ideally this would cover the whole city, but elsewhere it could comprise a number of endowed assets and resources. (See Principle 2)

- Participatory budgeting: The realisation of empowerment is participation (Principles 6 and 8)

- Clear values – sharing prosperity: Linked with rights, duties and responsibilities – The Garden City must be a place where the individual can flourish, it is also a place where the community comes together to take responsibility and is proud to share its prosperity to create enjoyment as well as to address poverty and social injustice. A key duty of the citizen is to be a trustee for the City and guardian of it rights and to ensure that it exercises its duties fairly. (See Principles 2,6,7,8,9,10 and 11)

- Links with land and access to resources: Linked with community ownership and is a manifestation of empowerment and citizenship to help the community develop and for the individual to flourish (See Principle 4)

- Training\induction\orientation for new people joining the Garden City so they understand the principles and can become active citizens (See also Principle 7)

Key Conclusions

- Citizenship is the glue that turns factories, houses, allotments, farms and gardens into communities

- Empowerment, not entitlement, is the goal

- Empowerment created through participation

- Participation is about scrutiny and governance

- Citizenship offers respect and suggests equality

- Citizenship is a way of letting people know that they are empowered

- Citizenship training and induction is important

- Citizenship is about not relying on the paternalism or charity of a benevolent monarch, council or government

- Participatory budgeting is a way to exercise active citizenship (See Principles 6 and 8)

[2] The Garden City owns itself

The Garden City is ultimately owned by its local community and not by a series of landlords. This ownership and governance is derived from the people who live and work in the city and who are its citizens acting for the common good. If the Garden City is its own landlord then it is answerable to and controlled by its citizens, ideally as a Community Land Trust managed by democratic structures that make it both inclusive and accountable.

This, along with pledges on participation, is the greatest and most powerful of all the pledges because it is a tangible realisation of citizenship. It is about the real and tangible ownership of the Garden City. It is about common and collective forms of tenure of the city and the assets within it. Ownership itself isn't enough, without active citizens capable of holding it to account it will not work. In some places in the world people want to participate but aren't allowed to and in other parts where they are encouraged to but people can't be bothered.

We believe that if people live in their own city and have a stake in its prosperity then that will help to engender the idea of citizenship, which is what Ebenezer Howard understood when he envisaged the first Garden City. The city was not to be a charity or something held in trust but about real common ownership. Nor is it about people holding just passive paper shares in the city speculating on its success but instead participating in it, building it, making it an 'oeuvre d'art' - a masterpiece sharing its success and shouldering its responsibilities as well.

How can this be done? How can people hold the land in common? There are many ways that residents can be their own landlords. This could be through a Co-operative model, through a community land trust or a co-operative land bank.

As far as garden cities are concerned there needs to be a mechanism so that residents can own and operate the Garden City for the common good.

Box 5. Nationalised Industries: Owned by the people?

In 1940s when some British industries were nationalised this was equated with public ownership for instance at the coal mines when signs went up saying 'These mines are now owned by the people'. But people didn't feel that they owned the mines or other nationalised industries. Margaret Thatcher said 'Ownership by the state is not the same as ownership by the people - it is the very opposite.

The owner of the city and its assets isn't a distant landlord, but neither is it the local council or central government. (See box 5). Nominally, the assets could be under control of the 'local council', but in the UK at least, people wouldn't trust the council to defend or protect those assets. For instance, many people believe that in Letchworth if the assets had been under control of the district council then they would have been sold off piecemeal over the years to fund lower taxes to gain political favour with voters. Instead, by locking the assets inside of a trust they have been kept together for the long term benefit – "in perpetuity" as the Common Land Trust slogans usually say.

Box 6. Garden Cities are more than just housing

An important point to remember is that our focus isn't just on the housing stock it is on the whole town: the agricultural land, the commercial and industrial space. In fact a Garden City is the opposite of a company town. A company town was where the factory provided homes for its workers. A Garden City is where the workers own the land that the company is based on - whether factory, agricultural or commercial.

The aim is to move this common ownership model from the small estate to truly being town and city-wide and ensure that social values are not replaced by bureaucratic or corporate ones. The co-operative movement can offer assistance here.

It is to be a system centred on people, on human beings and not on profit for a few or just on housing or land (See box 6). It will promote co-operatives for production of goods and housing and mutual-aid (mutualism) for health and security.

Community Land Trusts (CLT)

One of the most successful models of common land ownership is the CLT model. One model was originated in the United States by Ralph Borsodi and Robert Swann. They drew upon earlier examples of planned communities on leased land including Howard's Garden Cities, single tax communities in the USA, Gramdan villages in India (where wealthy landowners do voluntarily give a percentage of their land to lower castes. The idea was that this land was then held in common by the entire village). The prototype for the modern-day community land trust in the USA was formed in 1969 near Albany, Georgia by leaders of the southern civil rights movement.

The idea of a community land trust is that the land does effectively belong to the people that live and work on it. It is both a co-operative and Garden City principle and it is not just a hypothetical principle as it has been enacted successfully throughout the world. As of September 2013 there are over 200 CLT's in the USA and new ones are emerging in various places worldwide like Brussels in Belgium and Voi in Kenya.

An alternative to CLT's are Co-operative Land Banks, and these are discussed in box 9.

Box 7. Definitions of a Community Land Trust

Pat Conaty. Community Land Trusts have their origins in Britain: they are neither new nor imported. Common ownership of land, in which land is conceived of as a resource akin to air or water, was the historic norm.

Burlington CLT. CLT is a locally-controlled non-profit corporation created to serve as the permanent repository for a community's land and as the permanent steward for any residential or commercial buildings that are located upon its land. Land acquired by a community land trust is never resold, but is held forever in trust for the entire community.

CLT Network. The purposes of a Community Land Trust are to provide access to land and housing to people who are otherwise denied access; to increase long-term community control of neighbourhood resources; to empower residents through involvement and participation in the organization; and to preserve the affordability of housing permanently.

Building & Social Housing Foundation. A community Land Trust is a not-for-profit community controlled organisation that owns, develops and manages local assets for the benefit of the local community. Its objective is to acquire land and property and hold it in trust for the benefit of a defined locality or community in perpetuity (Deacon, Clarke et al. 2005).

Statutory Definition in the UK

In Britain, the statutory definition of a Community Land Trust (CLT) was added to the *Housing and Regeneration Act 2008*[4] during its progress through Parliament (See box 8 on British Housing Regeneration Act 2008).

The British Government has been supportive of the idea of community owned assets.

Housing Minister Grant Shapps announced in June 2010 of CLTs "the land will remain in the Trust for local benefit forever - regardless of what happens to the homes built on top. People have waited long enough for a model that is on their side rather than on the side of the bureaucrat. I want to unlock the passion and drive of these communities".[5]

Box 8. British Housing and Regeneration Act 2008

A Community Land Trust is a corporate body which:

[1] is established for the express purpose of furthering the social, economic and environmental interests of a local community by acquiring and managing land and other assets in order to provide a benefit to the local community to ensure that the assets are not sold or developed except in a manner which the trust's members think benefits the local community

[2] is established under arrangements which are expressly designed to ensure that:

any profits from its activities will be used to benefit the local community (otherwise than by being paid directly to members) individuals **who live or work** in the specified area have the opportunity to become members of the trust (whether or not others can also become members) the members of a trust control it.

Box 9. Co-operative Land Banks[6]

"Year by year, exclusive forms of ownership concentrate wealth in the hands of a few at the expense of the many. Year by year, the public debt load rises and private citizens suffer the consequences, including massive cuts in state subsidies for affordable housing. It is inefficient, it is unjust, and it has to change".

Shann Turnbull has designed a way to end this process. His **Co-operative Land Bank (CLB)** creates a way to reward private investment for commercial or industrial purposes in an area in the medium term, while diverting ownership, wealth, and responsibility into the hands of local residents over the long term.

He proposes that the ownership of the urban land base be separated from the ownership of buildings on the land. The land belongs to the CLB. Its shares are distributed to residents according to the area occupied by their dwelling (e.g., one share per square meter).

Ownership in a dwelling or commercial or industrial building takes the form of a transferable lease from the CLB. Whereas the leases on dwellings are perpetual, those for commercial or industrial buildings are time-limited; such investors retain ownership only until they recover their investments. Voting privileges in CLB deliberations are reserved to those who hold community shares.

Consequently, residents acquire equity in the entire site. Profits and rents are channelled to the CLB, which also captures the rise in land values due to public investment in infrastructure. It becomes self-financing. Incentive for entrepreneurship is preserved, while the machinery that enriches the few and marginalises the many is dislocated."

In the US, CLTs are committed not only to making housing affordable for income-eligible households, but also to maintaining the affordability in perpetuity and/or ensuring that any capital receipts are recycled within the local community. The first article of the City of Burlington, which gave birth to the major CLT in the USA, reads, "Housing is a right, not a commodity". Through CLT mechanism and the Champlain Housing Trust, they are delivering on this right.

Highland Park CLT in Illinois, USA has as its first principle to: "provide housing opportunities for low and moderate-income households that will permanently remain affordable for future generations"[7].

How do they work?

Basically a CLT separates the ownership of land from that of any property built on that land. The Community Land Trust retains ownership of the land whereas the properties built, houses, commercial buildings, restaurants, etc. on it can be leased, rented, or be of cooperative or individual properties.

We like the definition from Deacon and Clarke on how a CLT works, which reads as[8]:

"A CLT separates the value of the land from the buildings that stand on it and can be used in a wide range of circumstances to preserve the value of any public and private investment, as well as planning gain and land appreciation for community benefit. Crucially, local residents and businesses are actively involved in planning and delivering affordable local housing, workspace or community facility"

The CLT effectively leases the land to the homeowner or whoever is going to use it while the homeowner is effectively a shareholder in the CLT. It works the same for commercial property, the CLT owns the land and the business owns the building but pays lease costs to the CLT which generates income.

In Burlington, as the CLT owns the land it can build property more cheaply so often builds apartments with mixed tenancy, some owned privately and some owned by the housing association[9]. Alternatively, they may not own the land but simply own a number of apartments designated as affordable housing in a larger block.

When a resident comes to sell their apartment, they are entitled get back what they paid for it plus a maximum 25% benefit. So if someone bought an apartment for $100,000 and then 5 years later this same apartment is worth $200,000 on the market, he would only entitled to keep $125,000 the other $75,000 would go to the CLT. In practice this means that if a couple bought an apartment and years later their income had increased and they wanted to enter the property market, they may chose to leave the CLT. Others on lower incomes would remain secure. The CLT's have these assets which have risen in value and they use to maintain affordability for the new comers, as usually CLT properties have to be affordable for people below the local median income. Resources captured through this resale formula can be used by CLTs as collateral to borrow against to build or improve other assets.

Box 10. The Co-operative Land Bank: a Self-financing and Ownership Transfer System for Garden Cities.[10]

Where a CLB building is a block of flats, each tenant through their rent or lease payments would obtain co-ownership of their dwelling at the rate of, say, 4% per year. Co-ownership of all non-residential developments would be obtained by the CLB as they are written down for tax purposes. The rights to income would remain with the commercial owner. The accounting profits for the landlord would not change; the bottom line remains the same. At the end of the 25 years the ownership of all shopping precincts, offices, factories, entertainment facilities and all other non-residential developments would be 100% owned by the CLB. This limits surplus profits beyond the point where the private owner has recovered the costs of the building in full and enjoyed a competitive return on their investment.

The model notes that residents buy their homes by mortgaging their perpetual lease. If they rent it out at any time, the incoming tenant becomes a co-owner at, say, 4% per year. This provides an incentive for leaseholders to sell rather than to become an absentee landlord.

The flow of revenue to the CLB comes from three sources: a) residential rents and charges for services; b) commercial and industrial rates and leases that also capture any surplus profits; and c) from the trading in its own shares.

The unearned increment

Why bother with all this land ownership? The answer is all to do with land values and the fact that they continue to rise. The first Garden City was built on this principle so when writing about the revenue of the Garden City and how it might be obtained Howard said[11] :

> *Thus, while in some parts of London the rent is equal to £30,000 an acre, £4 an acre is an extremely high rent for agricultural land. This enormous difference of rental value is, of course, almost entirely due to the presence in the one case and the absence in the other of a large population; and, as it cannot be attributed to the action of any particular individuals, it is frequently spoken of as the 'unearned increment', i.e. unearned by the landlord, though a more correct term would be 'collectively earned increment'.*

> *The presence of a considerable population thus giving a greatly additional value to the soil, it is obvious that a migration of population on any considerable scale to any particular area will be certainly attended with a corresponding rise in the value of the land to settled upon, and it is also obvious that such increment of value may, with some foresight and pre-arrangement, become the property of the migrating people.*

> *Such foresight and pre-arrangement, never before exercised in an effective manner, are displayed conspicuously in the case of Garden City, where the*

land, as we have seen, is vested in trustees, who hold it in trust (after payment of the debentures) for the whole community, so that the entire increment of value gradually created becomes the property of the city, with the effect that though rents may rise, and even rise considerably, such rise in rent will not become the property of private individuals.

In Letchworth Garden City, the community land model still exists in modified form (See box 11). Burlington CLT has its own ownership model (see box 13).

However, note that both in Howard's time and in the present the increase of price is not only linked to what could be interpreted in the text as it is a demographic factor (more people). Pressure on land and very high level of demand implies that prices are increasing. On top of this speculators, anticipating this high demand are why land prices increase and are captured by a few landlords.

Capturing Land Values

Cost and value of land tends to continue to rise, while wages can remain stagnant or increase much less, the winners are those that hold the deeds to the land. Sometimes this value rises when the taxpayer invests money in improving the local infrastructure, yet it is property owners (and not tenants or leaseholders) who gain the most benefit. To illustrate this in the

USA it was reported that median housing values increased by 81% over the past 30 years whereas medium household incomes increased only by 24%.

Lewis and Turnball[12] in introducing their concept of Community Land Banks (see box 10) wrote a text that could have been penned in spirit by Ebenezer Howard one hundred years earlier:

The taxpayers of London, England invested £3.5 billion in the 1990's to extend the underground system. Following the completion of the Jubilee Line, property values within 1,000 yards of each of the eleven new stations jumped 3.7 times to £13 billion. Who benefitted from this windfall? Not average folks in Southwark, that is for sure. The spike in property values (which went up £9.5 billion) - and the rise in rents they justified - all went to landlords, most of them absentee, corporate owners. The wealth created by investment of taxpayers' money in the underground was sucked out of the community, right into the pockets of the wealthiest.

Box 11. Letchworth Garden City - Ownership model

Letchworth is the first garden city and was begun around 1903 and remains a key example of where an organisation still manages much of the Garden City estate. Unlike other schemes, it is the whole town that is nominally managed in this way as opposed to tracts of land or small areas. Over the years Letchworth has faced a number of challenges. Originally, the shares in the company that built and owned Letchworth were vested in residents, but by the 1960's the governance model was failing and some householders were willing to sell their shares to a corporate raider called Amy Rose. She tried to buy up all the shares in the town and was only thwarted by an Act of Parliament which effectively nationalised the town and its assets creating the Letchworth Garden City Corporation.

In the 1990's the Government 'privatised' the assets and created the Letchworth Garden City Heritage Foundation as a 'friendly society' to manage the estate going forward. It remains the major land owner in the town and retains 'quasi-public powers' for residential planning [13]applications.

But by 2009 it had declared itself to be a 'private property company like Grosvenor Estates in London' and it took High Court action to silence residents led by myself (Philip Ross as Mayor) who disputed this and regarded it as a community company and wanted it to be more democratic. The High Court ruled in our favour and now following a change of management the Foundation is back on course as a community focused organization.

Letchworth may no longer be exactly the sustainable, self-sufficient community that Howard envisaged and this is in part due to its proximity to London, (about 30 miles or 30 minutes by train), which means much of the population commute to the metropolis for work, but the result of such proximity has been increasing land values which have been captured by the trust that owns the assets. The wealth and success of Letchworth doesn't come down to the management of the Trust (in fact it was not run that well for a long time), but to the rising land values and it was able to capture this value. Today it is reported to have a book value (net asset value) of £127 million.

It is a charitable Industrial and Provident Society. Its mission is to generate income from its 5,500 acre property estate in order to fund charitable activities, including recreation and leisure, education and learning and the relief of poverty and sickness. It generates annual revenue of around £7 millions a year to spend in the town[14]. This money is spent running the organisation and on a local cinema, a community farm, a day hospital, subsidised transport, a local museum on Garden Cities, the tourist information and other services and also grants to many local organisations such as the local arts group, sports groups that need new equipment, to the 'Cheap as Chips' club that provides meals and support for the homeless and others. (See boxes 11, 13 for examples from Letchworth and Burlington and box 12 for more on Public Sector Land Banks).

Box 12. Public Sector Land Banks and Community Land Trust Partnerships[15]

John Stuart Mill's proposals in the 1850s for land nationalisation and other ways to 'capture the unearned increment' gave rise to proactive reforms pursued by local government. Mill was directly involved during his lifetime with successful campaigns in London to develop public parks and to preserve green spaces from commercial development. His proposals inspired the development of municipal socialism from the 1870s including public sector led projects for the provision of light, power and water. The work of Garden City architects, Barry Parker and Raymond Unwin revolutionised the approach to town planning and urban design. Letchworth showed how 'co-operative land tenure' enabled the unearned increment to be captured for community benefit. Could this approach be updated for re-designing towns and cities in the 21st century?

An exciting prospect is offered by the scope to link up public land bank and site assembly efforts to regenerate derelict urban areas with Community Land Trusts as a succession strategy. At present, the model is a public-private partnership, which allows 'windfalls and free lunches' to be earned by the private sector. A revived Garden City approach can ensure housing affordability over the long-term and can capture the 'unearned increment' for the benefit of local citizens. Shann Turnbull's updated Garden City model based on the development of Co-operative Land Banks could be 'win-win' as it would enable private development finance to be harnessed through an ownership transfer arrangement structured and repaid equitably by avoiding the yield of 'surplus profits' in perpetuity. The CLT movement in the USA is in dialogue with local authorities to find ways to trial Public Land Bank and CLT Partnerships. As John Emmeus Davis argues, CLTs have a land acquisition problem in cities that impedes their expansion while public sector agencies have a land disposition problem following their work on 'removing contaminants, clearing title and readying sites for redevelopment.' CLTs can solve the disposition problem. There is an evident strategic opportunity for securing a complete paradigm shift with such a dynamic public-social partnership approach.

Taken from Conaty, P. and Large, M. (2013) Common Sense - Cooperative place making and the capturing of land value for 21st century Garden Cities, Co-operatives UK Limited.

Box 13. Burlington CLT in Vermont, USA

The Champlain Housing Trust, founded in 1984 with capital of $200,000, by 2010 it had assets worth $40m. It is the largest community land trust in the USA. Throughout Chittenden, Franklin and Grand Isle counties, CHT manages 1,500 apartments, stewards over 500 owner-occupied homes and provides homebuyer education and financial counselling in its signature shared-equity program, provides services to five housing cooperatives and offers affordable energy efficiency and rehab loans. In 2008, CHT won the prestigious United Nations World Habitat Award, recognising its innovative, sustainable programs

It was an early pioneer of the Community Land Trust approach of providing affordable housing in perpetuity. CHT's homes are, on average, affordable to households earning only 57 per cent of the area's median income and it has over 2,200 properties for low-cost home ownership and rental. Over 200 community land trusts have now been established throughout the United States, with pilot schemes currently being carried out in both Canada and the UK.

Common land ownership – What should happen in practice

The city is owned by the people who live or work in it, or simply use it. Different mechanisms are available to enable this to happen such as -

- Co-operative ownership

- Community land trust

- Community land bank

The type of ownership will differ from the land to what is built on it or provided by it. Ownership is only one step. Management and accountability are crucial for this to succeed, in fact, to fail on the governance could mean that the Garden City could fail to be accountable to anyone and could become the worst and not the best landlord. (See Principles 6, 7 and 8)

Key Conclusions

A community land trust is by its very nature, accountable to the people that inhabit it. It is therefore of the upmost importance that the governance and management of the trust is fair and equitable otherwise it can quite easily move from being a socially engaged organisation to be at best, a paternalistic one and at worst, a neo-feudal one that exercises control but it is not accountable. If the Community Land Trust is not held to account or can be dominated by a small group then it has failed, it becomes not the landlord of the people, for people but of people.

Ownership is only part of the story, it will need good management for the long term and democratic governance otherwise it will just become a 'super' landlord.

A Community land trust without democratic governance and scrutiny is the worst of all landlords.

In summary:

- Tangible realisation of citizenship and a stake in society

- If you can own the land or the town then need mechanisms to hold them to account

- If nobody is accountable then the trust can become the worst landlord of all

[3] The Garden City is energy efficient and carbon neutral

A Garden City has a harmonious relationship with nature and is energy efficient. A Garden City is a carbon neutral city and does not pollute. It's planning, design and resources are deployed to achieve this goal. Citizens and the Government in the Garden City have a collective responsibility in their daily lives to design and implement such policies and practices. This could be ensuring the provision of clean, safe and efficient public transport, the ability to navigate the Garden City by walking or cycling on one hand and the ability to reduce waste, recycle and reuse resources by citizens on the other.

A Garden City has a harmonious relationship with nature and the countryside. As such, it aims to be energy efficient and aware of its carbon footprint.

Ebenezer Howard sought to bring the best of town and country together. He sought to combine the health of the country with the benefits of the town. That objective remains as true and as important for the New Garden City Movement as it did for Howard in 1903. Back then, Howard wrote about murky skies in the cities and clean air in the country. In parts of the developing world, this remains an issue.

> *"... by so laying out a Garden City that, as it grows, the free gifts of Nature- fresh air, sunlight, breathing room and playing room- shall be still retained in all needed abundance" (Garden Cities of To-morrow, 1902 edition, page 113)*

When visiting Chengdu, the capital of Sichuan province in China, in 2012, one of the people we met was inspired to say that he understood garden cities to be about 'Ruralising the town!' not urbanising the countryside. It is a good slogan and one that Howard would probably have been at home with.

The Garden City seeks to be a city of rights and with rights. A key right is the right to clean air and this is one of the reasons why this principle is so important. While it can be relatively easier to build in a carbon neutral infrastructure into a new city (see for instance Masdar City on-going project, Abu Dhabi) but that doesn't mean that existing cities cannot retrofit such policies themselves.

Throughout much of the world, the argument is being won on climate change and for those living with the murky skies that Ebenezer Howard experienced, the need for action is even clearer. To some this is clean energy, to others it is recycling and reuse.

The principles of garden cities and the need for citizenship and use of land for urban agriculture, these values dovetail nicely with the aim to be carbon neutral. (See Principles 1 and 4). Sympathetic design that is people friendly often suggests easy travel by inter-connected public transport and by foot and bike as opposed to just by car.

It is possible to retrofit such a travel system into an existing city. For instance, Hong Kong has the high walk, which integrates in with their mass transit system. It is easy to travel round the city by foot as it is by car or taxi. This has been retrofitted into the city.

The ultimate objective of this principle is to provide pathways for urban development with low energy consumption, low pollution, low emissions, high energy efficiency and high benefit to society.

Adding Green Policies

While schemes such as in Masdar (see box 14), Dezhou and the plans for the Great City in Chengdu[16] show that it is possible to build with green policies from the start, the question remains of how such policies can fit into existing cities.

Box 14. Masdar as a carbon free city[17]

Masdar city is a planned city near Abu Dhabi in the United Arab Emirates. It is being constructed to be a zero carbon city and will rely on solar energy and other renewable energy sources with a zero waste and zero carbon ecology. It will be a 'car free' city.

Though a 'carbon free city' it is not what we would call a Garden City, it demonstrates that the technology to produce such a city of the future is largely available today.

The Transition Towns Movement (see box 15) is starting to answer this question by focusing on how to make existing towns more environmentally sustainable. Much can be done to conserve energy, find new sources of energy and to reuse and recycle.

The garden city perspective shares this principle but remember that a garden city is people centred and not landscape or building centred.

Box 15. What are Transitions Towns? [18]

They are community-led movements whose main aim is to raise awareness of sustainable living and build local strategies to deal with the challenges of peak oil and climate change. The result is a growing number of communities worldwide developing local food networks, local energy supplies, local transport and even local money.

The movement was originally popularised by permaculture expert Rob Hopkins, based in Totnes in the UK. "The idea of transition towns has caught people's imagination," he explained. "All we have been able to do before is protest, lobby or campaign for change. Now we want to give people the tools to be self-sufficient and withstand the kind of shock that a reduction in oil would bring. We don't have all the answers, but the amount of momentum and energy created by the project is amazing."

Carbon Neutral City - What should happen in practice

To build or develop a carbon neutral city is not easy but examples do exist where new cities are being built to such standards. There are small developments elsewhere that can achieve this. To clear the murky skies the key focus must be on the motor car. The car remains a potent symbol of prosperity and wealth and there is the need to overcome both cultural and economic obstacles.

Positive assistance can be given to low-income households with positive results such as the 'green mortgages' example above illustrates, public transport can both use renewable energy and preserve energy as well as curb pollution.

How can a Garden City with little wind, little sun, obtain renewable energy? One way is that the community could choose to use any dividend that the city develops to fund the purchase of green energy into the town or city or to invest in geo-thermal energy (See box 16).

Key Conclusions

- Garden City should be carbon neutral.

- Green transport built-in with cycle lanes.

- Avoids heat waves in the city.

- Designed for access by foot and bicycle.

- It should have a neutral effect on the surrounding district.

- The city processes all its own waste and rubbish and promotes reuse and recycling.

- The Garden City promotes urban agriculture with an aim of ruralising the town and increasing food sovereignty.

Box 16. What is District heating?

District heating is a system for distributing heat generated in a centralised location for residential and commercial heating requirements, such as space heating and water heating. The heat is often obtained from a cogeneration plant burning fossil fuels but increasingly biomass, although heat-only boiler stations, geothermal heating and central solar heating are also used as well as nuclear power. District heating plants can provide higher efficiencies and better pollution control than localised boilers.

According to some research, district heating with combined heat and power is the cheapest method of cutting carbon emissions and has one of the lowest carbon footprints of all fossil generation plants. This approach is being developed in Denmark as a store for renewable energy, particularly wind electric, that exceeds instantaneous grid demand via the use of heat pumps and thermal stores.[19]

[4] Provide access to the land for living and working to all

The Garden City promotes urban agriculture, the ability for citizens to grow most of their own food, even in an urban area. There is a right of free and fair access to the land for all residents to grow their own food whether it is through common allotments, common land, farms, productive streets and parks or private gardens. Alongside this is the right to affordable housing and also the right of access to resources in urban areas to build or run their individual or collective businesses or workshops. It is a productive city that aims at its own self-sufficiency providing opportunities for agricultural work, crafts, commerce and industry. Affordable rents are provided to encourage self-sufficiency and regeneration, provided in partnership with tenants, not just for tenants. The goal is for the City to be productive and sustainable in its own right, not as a dormitory settlement or a city that consumes without producing, as most do.

Land, it comes down to land and access to the land for homes, for food and for commerce and industry. When we originally devised this principle, our focus was on urban agriculture and the growing of food whether in allotments, gardens, roof gardens, balconies or vertical gardens. Urban agriculture had been a key part of Howard's original blueprint. His focus was on a ring of farms around the town and for large gardens and allotments, but the issue is land and its access for housing, for business or industry and for public usage.

Housing

While it is a tenet of the Garden City philosophy for the common-ownership of the city by its residents, this does not preclude the private or cooperative ownership of properties built on the land owned by the CLT. In terms of housing, we would expect there to be private or community owned properties on commonly owned land. The Garden City will own the land and the individuals or families will own their properties (Principle 2).

A Garden City should use its wealth and prosperity to provide affordable housing for its residents and citizens that are safe, clean and secure. Freedom from crime is an important tenet and Garden Cities responsibility is to provide a safe and secure environment at home and at work (For an example see box 17).

Box 17. Housing Co-operatives in Uruguay

FUCVAM[20] is a federation of mutual aid housing cooperatives and is the largest, oldest and most active social movement working on issues of housing and urban development in Uruguay and have produced thousands of homes. In 2001, a South-South Cooperation project was initiated to support the international transfer of the FUCVAM approach – which follows the key principles of solidarity, democratic participation, self-management, mutual aid and collective ownership of property – to other countries in the region and around the world. FUCVAM has transferred the approach to 15 countries across Latin America, adapting the model to local conditions in different contexts, setting up national federations and networks.

Small business, craftsman and local resources

Commerce and the individual should flourish in the Garden City. A key resource is land and rents and it is clearly within the remit of the Garden City to provide affordable rents and additional services to help the city develop and sustain itself. For instance, this could mean cheaper offices or workshops or it could mean free city-wide internet as a normal basic service. Today's craftsmen may be small internet firms or others engaged in commerce. As well as providing cheaper rents, the Garden City can also share its prosperity with new firms. For instance, by offering loans in a local currency or even creating a form of crowd financing.

Residents could all receive a dividend from the Garden City but in the form of a local currency. They could choose to spend it locally, pay their taxes with some of it, or invest in local businesses. Local firms could put out prospectuses for loans and investment. This could follow the model as done by UK peer-to-peer lender Zopa yet it could be the Garden City that administers this (See Principle 6). Just as families may come together to help each other start a business the Garden City community should do the same by providing access to the resources to allow this to happen. The use of a local currency can help to retain prosperity in the city that is subsequently generated as a pre-condition of Garden City finance.

Urban Agriculture

A Garden City will promote urban agriculture, the ability for citizens to grow their own food, raise fish and other animals in an urban area. The right of free and fair access to the land for all residents to grow their own food or food for sale whether it be through common allotments, common land or in private gardens is crucial (See box 18).

Box 18. Urban Agriculture

The most striking feature of urban agriculture, which distinguishes it from rural agriculture, is that it is integrated into the urban economic and ecological system: urban agriculture is embedded in -and interacting with- the urban ecosystem. Such linkages include the use of urban residents as labourers, use of typical urban resources (like organic waste as compost and urban wastewater for irrigation), direct links with urban consumers, direct impacts on urban ecology (positive and negative), being part of the urban food system, competing for land with other urban functions, being influenced by urban policies and plans, etc. Urban agriculture is not a relic of the past that will fade away (urban agriculture increases when the city grows) nor brought to the city by rural immigrants that will lose their rural habits over time. It is an integral part of the urban system.[21]

A key tenet of a Garden City is free, open and fair access to the land. If we agree that citizenship is about people having a stake in their society, feeling part of their community and sharing sovereignty of it, then a key manifestation of that is free access to the land. It is considered to be a right in a Garden City.

Having access to the land takes two forms, firstly for recreation and secondly for cultivation. Obviously, city parks and gardens will always form a part of this, space for sports and recreations. Uncultivated land is also vital though, for walking, visiting and gradual expansion of the Garden City. Land can cultivate more than just food; it can also cultivate health and happiness in its citizens. Open access to the land brings a feeling of freedom and liberty.

There is also a worldwide movement to promote urban agriculture – the growing of food in our towns and cities, not just in the countryside. It is natural territory for any aspiring Garden City. A Garden City should be actively promoting and enabling this to happen. In Britain, there is a history and tradition of garden allotments. These are smallholdings of land allocated to city dwellers where they can grow their own crops of vegetables or even just harvest their own plants. The key point about the garden allotments is that they don't need to be a car journey away or in another town or village, as can be the case on the continent. Allotments were created in 18th century England as a way of alleviating the distress of the rural poor. At the same time, allotments were unfortunately promoted as a way to keep workers away from trade unions, from local pubs and other supposed "evils" generated by the city. The English countryside had gradually been enclosed, which meant that many small, scattered land holdings had been consolidated into a lesser number of holding in the hands of a few wealthy landowners.[22]

Box 19. Community Land Trusts and Local Food

---

1. Intervale in Burlington, Vermont: has developed a scheme for local food on 200 acres of dumping ground (6ft of rubbish) – now a 'city garden' of a dozen community farms supplying 7% fresh food for a town of 35,000.

2. Evergreen Co-ops in Cleveland, Ohio: Green City Growers – largest city farm in the USA with 5.5 acre greenhouse growing 6 million of lettuce and 300,000 pounds of herbs yearly through a worker co-op in the city's poorest inner city area.

3. Community Land Advisory Service: new project of the National Federation of City Farms and Gardens and now underway in England and Scotland to create Community Land Banks for food growing in cities, towns and villages.

It isn't always possible to provide allotments for everyone but instead, common or shared ground or land should be made available. Cities in South America have provided old waste or unused land which they have handed over for communal use (See box 19).

Box 20. Urban Agriculture in Letchworth Garden City

In Letchworth 100 years ago, in common with other enlightened towns, homes were provided with large gardens with which to grow their own vegetables. Due to space restrictions and lack of land such generous gardens are unlikely to feature in house estates now. Indeed in some towns people have successfully sold off their gardens and allowed further homes to be built. In Letchworth this practice was outlawed.

Letchworth was designed with a ring of farms surrounding it (about half the estate was agricultural and still is), in the hope that it would make the town self-sufficient in food. (Though 100 years later some have been sold off or don't operate agriculturally, but the concept and principle remains true). The remaining farm (the green belt remains) does operate but it doesn't operate to supply the town directly with food but supplies the national market in general. This is a comment on modern agriculture; Letchworth doesn't have the capacity to mill corn and the like. It did experiment with a local store selling local meat and produce. The quality was good but it failed economically and closed. However, the local Horticultural society, which was found in 1904 and is still active, do have their own shop for selling seeds, tools and pesticides. Half the estate is under cultivation and allotments group are thriving, and this is unique.

The Letchworth town council in 2008-9 continued this trend; it was instrumental in helping new community gardens be set up in the Jackmans and Grange estates. These gardens went hand in hand with the creation and support of local neighbourhood councils, it in effective worked to create a feeling of citizenship and belonging, that some local space can be fashioned by the community. Other projects included plans to take over the allotments and hand over their management to the allotment holders association, not as a measure to absolve the council of responsibility for them but to empower the allotment holders themselves. Similarly, gardening tools and equipment were provided for local groups who wished to take over allotments.

Access to the land in Action

Cuban experience in urban agriculture

In Cuba, because of the American blockage and the collapse of the Soviet Union, the Cuban industrial agricultural policy was in jeopardy, largely through a lack of oil and petrol to run the huge farms they had - that had previously been used for sugar cane production, which had been exhausting the land. Cuba was in crisis and went through a period known as the 'special period' during which a nationwide famine was a distinct possibility. Cuba had to find a new way to survive and put a focus on sustainable agriculture and a need to reduce the use of automobiles. (Ironically, this is something the whole of the western world is trying to accomplish).

The result is now that Cuba is the world leader in urban agriculture with the cities and towns growing masses of food within their boundaries, all spare space is put over to food production (See box 21). It is a little how London became during the Second World War when the 'dig for victory' campaign was running. Much of this success is done to the fact that people have co-operated and shared their knowledge, their know-how and innovations (See Principle 11).

Box 21. Havana, Cuba, a world leader in urban agriculture[23]

When the Soviet Bloc collapsed in 1989, Cuba lost its food imports and agricultural inputs from which it depended for an adequate supply of food. The US Embargo also created a shortage of petrol necessary to transport the food from the rural agriculture sector to the city. This marked the beginning of serious food shortages that shook the entire country, but most of all Havana.

When these sources where cut off and food shortages began, Havana residents responded en masse, planting food crops on porches, balconies, backyards and empty city lots. The Cuban Ministry of Agriculture and Havana's city government supported this grassroots movement, jointly forming an Urban Agriculture Department in 1994. This department first focused on securing access to land for urban gardeners and committed itself to provide land - free of charge - to all residents who wanted to grow food in the city. Today, the government advice and disseminate knowledge is based on the principles of organic agriculture and usually plays a pivotal role in the start-up and functioning of the popular gardens and horticulture clubs. They also operate centres, selling agricultural supplies like seeds.

Access to land - What should happen in practice

We do not see the Garden City as being a single company town for workers in one factory; neither do we see it just as a pleasant suburb for social housing or as a government town. We see garden cities as being hot beds of entrepreneurial activity, a place where new businesses and the social economy (which is not focused on individual profit but on collective benefit) can begin and grow. Access to land for new companies to develop and grow as well as places where artisans can be secure is an important tenet of the Garden City philosophy.

Garden Cities are not just about housing, they are about land and providing access to it and generating income from it.

- Provision of allotments

- Low rent units

- Share facilities (e.g. Wi-Fi)

- Shared company services to support growing firms

- Identification of land ownership

- Register or land bank of unused land

- Provision of fruit orchards and availability of land for growing food, fish and animals

- Provision of plants produced locally for medicines

- Encouragement of allotments for recreation

- Establish an educational city farm to keep the urban-rural link for children

Key Conclusions

Providing access to the land is a key manifestation of citizenship and demonstrates a stake in the town. By giving people access to land for homes, or for commerce or business, or to grow food, it needs to be accompanied with duties and responsibilities, not just entitlement.

As the city is providing help with land for housing, business and growth, which should help the individual and family to flourish, then the bargain is that the prosperity generated is shared with the Garden City. The keys tenets need to be that:

- Access to land and to services and to homes

- Provide fair opportunity for all to start a business and to prosper

- Urban agriculture helps to balance sustainability of the GC.

- Makes the town a productive city

- An enabling principle, that the Garden City be a place for innovation, creativity and development

- That opportunity is open to all

The aim through this access to land is to help make the Garden City a vibrant community and not a dormitory town. Access to the land is a key and a mandatory tenet of any Garden City. A community seeking Garden City status could follow the fine examples set by Rosario in Argentina, Governador Valadares in Brazil and Cienfuegos in Cuba of using green mapping methods to identify unused cultivatable land.

A council or government administration should ensure that access to the land is in the fabric of their policymaking as it will help:

- Localised food production

- Empowers individuals to feel part of the community

- Builds commitment and purpose, especially for those retired or out of work

- Provides a sense of place for those living in flats with no land of their own.

[5] Fair Trade principles are practised

The Garden City is committed to the practises and ethics of Fair Trade implementing the credo that it's prosperity is not built upon the suffering of others, whether inside its own city limits, inside its own country or internationally.

A Garden City does not want its prosperity built upon the suffering of its own residents or those outside its borders. It actively believes in fair trade and its purchasing and trading policies reflect this.

The Fair Trade movement is sweeping across the western world as consumers realise that they have the power in their pockets to change the world. Their purchasing decisions and choices affect, for good or ill, the lives and futures of people across the planet.

Indeed Martin Luther King once said that when a man eats his breakfast he has already involved half of the world. The solution for the defeat of poverty isn't charity and paternalism from the west and elsewhere, but fair and ethical trading. It is grassroots power that has brought about this change so far, supermarket owners were sceptical that people would be willing to pay that little bit extra just because it was 'supposedly' ethical. But church and poverty campaigners faced them down and said, "Yes, people will". More people joined the cause and it is now becoming embarrassing for some firms, for instance coffee bars, not to be fair trade.

The principle of Fair Trade is an important one for a Garden City because it is about declaring and believing in the credo that its prosperity should not be built upon the suffering of others.

The Fair Trade movement may have started with tea and coffee and then moved to bananas but it is now extending to cotton and other products. In 2011 Bolivia became the first country to produce fair trade gold.

Fair Trade isn't just about paying a fair price it is about how ethically those goods are produced. It means that those producing have trade union rights, adequate health and safety and the knowledge that the fair trade dividend will be invested in their communities for the good of all. In effect, the Garden City principle is that prosperity should be shared.

Fair Trade Premium - Sharing Prosperity

Fair trade is more than just a fair price paid to producers, as well as pre-payment of part of the price it also includes an annual social premium- this premium is controlled by the producer co-operative and is spent on ways to enhance the entire producer community, whether that be by buying scales for coffee growers to stop them being underpaid by buyers or introducing basic pension schemes for retired workers. The Social Premium is a crucial part of the whole fair trade approach as it assists in future economic development and building sustainable communities. This is very much a Garden City ideal and shows the strong links between the two movements (See Principle 6).

Fair Trade Discussion

That people should get a fair price for their labour and their goods is what people have spent hundreds of years struggling for in Europe, through revolution, reform and more recently, consumer pressure.

True freedom can only be ensured if people have economic freedom and security. We can make common cause with that because when Letchworth was founded 100 years ago Ebenezer Howard declared it as a key tenet that the town should not have an over-arching landlord, but that the town should belong to its citizens and should share its own prosperity. The Fair Trade Foundation aims to give farmers from developed and developing countries a fair deal. Its mission statement is:

"Our vision is of a world in which justice and sustainable development are at the heart of trade structures and practices so that everyone, through their work, can maintain a decent and dignified livelihood and develop their full potential.

To achieve this vision, Fairtrade seeks to transform trading structures and practices in favour of the poor and disadvantaged. By facilitating trading partnerships based on equity and transparency, Fairtrade contributes to sustainable development for marginalised producers, workers and their communities.

Through demonstration of alternatives to conventional trade and other forms of advocacy, the Fairtrade movement empowers citizens to campaign for an international trade system based on justice and fairness."

The Fair Trade premium or social premium is a tangible way of sharing prosperity like that envisaged by Howard in Letchworth. It is a key Garden City principle.

We have the power in our pockets to make a difference. Fair trade doesn't have to be international either; we can begin at home ensuring our farmers get a fair price for their goods. We can insist, as consumers, on only buying goods and produce that has been ethically and environmentally friendly in its production.

While supporting the international principles of fair trade which apply between a first world and developing nation, the principle of fair trade needs to be a applied for local purchases too.

Box 22. Letchworth Garden City: a Fair Trade town since 2009

"Our focus ranged from everyday things like bananas, oranges, wine, tea, coffee, to the bigger things like the marble for the new town centre development. For example, one of our councillors in Letchworth pushed hard to argue that any raw materials purchased are both ethically and environmentally sourced. There is no point in people buying their fair trade coffee if they find themselves sitting on marble that was quarried by children on slave wages"[24].

In the UK towns, if they follow and fulfil a set of criteria, can apply to become 'fair trade towns'. This isn't just a council initiative but comes from the voluntary groups, charities, the churches and individuals in the town who have all been working hard to this end over the last year. In a Garden City the ethics and values of Fair Trade should be strong such that it is the expected behaviour.

Fair Trade - What should happen in practice

We would expect a Garden City to be also a Fair Trade City. It should promote ethical purchases for its citizens and the municipality and the Garden City administration should have fair trade ethics at the heart of purchasing policy for both raw materials and consumables and all goods. The Garden City should be carbon neutral and the aim should be to source materials locally where it can.

If there are local environmental assets the Garden City should seek to protect them from predators by accrediting them with environmental schemes such as the **Programme for the Endorsement of Forest Certification, PEFC (see box 23)**. It should support the PEFC scheme when making its own purchases.[25]

Box 23. The Programme for the Endorsement of Forest Certification, PEFC

PEFC is an international non-profit, non-governmental organization dedicated to promoting Sustainable Forest Management through independent third-party certification.

Key Conclusions

- Fair trade principle instilled into the Garden City and its citizens

- Prosperity not built on suffering of others

- An ethical city, cements in the other principles

- Not a closed community but an international one

- Aware not just of its carbon footprint but of how its trade affects others

21st Century Garden Cities of To-morrow

[6] Prosperity is Shared

The prosperity of the Garden City is shared in practise among all its citizens, not just among the rich, wealthy and establishment. Participatory budgeting through which citizens decide on the priorities for public and community investment is one of the key mechanisms in practise. To secure the wealth and trigger jobs among the community it can create local or a complementary community currency and set up community banks.

It is the purpose of a Garden City to address inequalities and in part redistribute wealth by sharing the town's prosperity with everyone.

In the Garden City much of the land that the housing, factories and business are built on and the fields that are farmed are owned by the Garden City as a community land trust or similar. This was discussed before under the heading 'the Garden City owns itself' (Principle 2), the consequence of this ownership is that it should be able to generate its own revenue from these commercial holdings[26]. If nothing else the rise in land values (the unearned increment) can be captured for the good of the community as opposed to this value going to absentee landlords. If the Garden City can secure such prosperity, the question follows on how is it to be spent and invested. Who makes these decisions and how is it to be done?

The governance of the Garden City is crucial. We have declared that the Garden City is commonly \mutually owned in the private sector or in what we would like to call the 'community sector' which is neither public nor private. (As opposed to being owned by the council).

The Garden City's prosperity is to be shared fairly among the population residing or using it and invested fairly for the future and wellbeing of the city. But what makes a Garden City different isn't just that this prosperity is to be shared, but how it is shared, who decides who it is shared between and how it is secured for the future (See Principle 8).

After all a charitable trust could hold the land and a committee of 'worthy' residents could determine what they consider to be worthwhile projects and schemes and hand out grants to grateful residents, just as a housing association could provide affordable homes. But this charitable and paternalistic model isn't the Garden City model. The Garden City model is about empowerment, participation and citizenship. The way that any Garden City dividend is spent or invested needs to reinforce those principles (See Principle 8).

Along with shared ownership of the city this is one the most important tenets of the Garden City. The wealth and prosperity generated by the Garden City, the common treasury that is the city, (to paraphrase Gerrard Winstanley who led the Diggers Movement in England following the Civil War in 1649 and founded an early community based on common ownership)[27] needs to be shared and shared in practice among all its citizens, not just by and for the rich and wealthy.

Profit for the Garden City

Cities do not exist as businesses – though they may conduct business activities and provide services. For instance, the collection of residential rubbish cannot be based on the ability to pay but has to be done for the common good. Previously we have discussed the concept of the city 'owning itself' and that citizenship with its sense of belonging and empowerment, comes from that. The activities that the city performs, the way it treats its residents and the services it provides are derived from a mandate and a set of principles – in this case the Garden City principles.

The opposite of profit is a loss and it is discussed in box 24 how Letchworth Garden City coped when it was running at a loss.

The Garden City is thus a place for individuals and collectives to flourish at the same time, not conform.

In Howard's second Garden City, Welwyn, the co-operative principle was applied across into retail. A 'common store' was established that people could shop in and it would keep the prices low and reinvest in the town. Other examples could be common-ownership of local energy, whether to generate green energy or to capture heat from existing sources.

Box 24. Sharing the debt - Letchworth Garden City

The flip side of a successful Garden City is one that is failing and may need to ask residents for financial support. Letchworth Garden City found itself in this situation in the 1980s. All residents were charged a special tax to support the estate called the 'Letchworth precept' although this was enforced as a tax as opposed to a voluntary contribution. Residents all recalled paying the tax, even though the later management of the Garden City estate had all but forgotten about it as they insisted that the 'Foundation costs residents nothing'. However, the mere fact that people did have to pay the extra tax in support strengthened their sense of ownership, or rather their disillusionment with it. Interestingly when land values rose and the Garden City came back into profit the precept was not repaid to residents. Many of course may have moved or left the Garden City. If though the precept had been collected in the form of a bond then it would have been possible to repay it and also strengthen the Garden City model.

Guiding Values

In conventional business, shareholders draw a dividend from having a financial stake and share in a company. In good times they make a profit and in bad times they may have to contribute more to save their investment. The same can be true for the Garden City model. It is about people having a social stake in their town and drawing a social dividend or making a social investment in terms of time or money. So for sharing prosperity the guiding principles must be:

- Sharing the prosperity fairly

- Participation in the decision making process - who makes the decisions

- Retaining prosperity in the Garden City

For the Garden City, co-operative and mutual values must be applied to support the first principle. Participatory budgeting is used to implement the second and local\alternative currencies and other policies can be used to support the third.

We believe that these objectives can be achieved by adherence to the Garden City principles and introducing a participatory model for decision-making and a local\alternate currency to retain profits in the city. The aim should be to empower communities and drive enterprise in the city, such that the city isn't just successful through its land values but through its generation of wealth for the common good.

Box 25. What is Participatory Budgeting?

Participatory Budget[28] is "a mechanism (or process) through which the population decides on, or contributes to decisions made on, the destination of all or part of the available public resources."

Ubiratán de Souza, one of the primary people responsible for the Participatory Budget in Porto Alegre (Brazil) proposes a more precise and theoretical definition that can be applied to the majority of the Brazilian cases: "Participatory Budgeting is a process of direct, voluntary and universal democracy, where the people can debate and decide on public budgets and policy. The citizen's participation is not limited to the act of voting to elect the executive or the legislators, but also decides on spending priorities and controls the management of the government. He ceases to be an enabler of traditional politics and becomes a permanent protagonist of public administration. The PB combines direct democracy with representative democracy, an achievement that should be preserved and valued.

In fact, the Participatory Budget is a form of participatory democracy, in other words a combination of elements of direct or semi-direct democracy with representative democracy.

Co-operative Principles

It is not a new idea for a business to provide dividends to its members and member owned societies, such as the co-operative retailer in the UK were famous for doing for generations.

The Co-operative Movement[29] began in England in the second half of the industrial revolution. It was driven partly by the loss of the common use of land as workers had nothing to sell but their labour. With no controls or rights, labour was plentiful and cheap, it was an age of child labour, exploitation and poverty and those who failed to find work in the new factories were forced to rely on meagre parish relief for the poor or to starve. During the early part of the century, the early 1800's, Robert Owen, a Welshman who made his fortune in cotton, tried to establish co-operative communities. These early experiments in creating complete mini-communities foundered but Owen identified some of the profound underlying values of co-operation as a means of organising economic activity. A little later, strikes by the weavers in Rochdale had failed to have any lasting effect on wages and living conditions so the weavers turned to the ideas of Owen and William King. With 28 members they started the first successful co-operative enterprise, the Rochdale Equitable Pioneer Society and also set up the first consumer co-operative in a shop. They started trading on 21st Dec 1844 selling the basic necessities of life to their members, butter, candles, soap, flour and blankets. Their aim was to supply good quality goods cheaply and to return any profit to members of the co-operative. They worked out that to succeed their co-operative enterprise must work on 7 key co-operative principles (see box 26). These are now recognised internationally as the 7 Co-operative Principles and remain the practical foundation of housing and other types of co-operative today.

Box 26. Co-operative principles and values

A co-operative is an autonomous association of persons united voluntarily to meet their common economic, social, and cultural needs and aspirations through a jointly-owned and democratically controlled enterprise. Co-operatives are based on the values of self-help, self-responsibility, democracy, equality, equity and solidarity. In the tradition of their founders, co-operative members believe in the ethical values of honesty, openness, social responsibility and caring for others.

[1] Voluntary and Open Membership

[2] Democratic Member Control

[3] Member Economic Participation

[4] Autonomy and Independence

[5] Education, Training and Information

[6] Co-operation among Co-operatives

[7] Concern for Community

The co-operative movement suggests shared ownership of business by the work force. In the British retail co-operative company the shareholder is in effect the customer. Customers are 'members' and generate a dividend based on their spending. In the 21st century there may seem to be a blurred line between this and a supermarket rewards card like those issued by Sainsbury's and Tesco's in the UK. In the same way there are Building Societies - mutualised credit unions run on co-operative lines – organisations that encouraged saving and made loans for homebuyers. There were/are no shareholders - those that participate in the business by saving or borrowing are the members, or in other words the owners of these mutual organisations, there are no shareholders.

The difference between the Garden City management model as opposed to one of local government is that the Garden City model isn't maintained by local taxation. It is actually a local company that operates as a not for profit business in the city and aims to generate social benefits that can be released to the local community. This may or may not be a simple monetary equation.

Shareholders in the Garden City have the right to participate in the strategic direction of the city and in how wealth is generated, invested and spent. There is of course a democratic deficit if shareholders can't do this and can't hold the management of the Garden City to account.

The downside is that companies aren't by their nature built as democratic institutions, though shareholders will shout to protect their investments, which is particularly true for big shareholders with big stakes, but for small shareholders they can be virtually powerless. Powerless shareholders can lead to bad governance as management can't be held to account.

Sharing of prosperity must be accountable and open to scrutiny, otherwise the result could be huge amounts being lavished on a 'private golf club' while just crumbs are allocated to real community projects.

Local prosperity

The point is that the prosperity or wealth that has been generated by the Garden City hasn't been generated out of thin air, nor usually has it come from some far off investments; it has actually been raised within the limits of the city itself and from those residents and businesses that call it home.

It makes sense then for the profits to be reinvested back into the community, and another good practice will be to use local firms to do this work and in doing so the money is virtuously recycled through the community again and again. One way to do this is through the introduction of a local\alternate currency which will lock value and prosperity into the city.

Box 27. How prosperity is shared in Letchworth

Letchworth Garden City was founded in 1903 when Ebenezer Howard led a group that bought a tract of land in Hertfordshire. He was supported by capital from philanthropic lenders such as the Cadbury Corporation. The company that was founded to build the town and manage the estate has changed its name and ownership model and governance over the years, but the estate has been held together. Today the company that operates it is called the Letchworth Garden City Heritage Foundation and it is a non-profit making Industrial and Provident Society.

As a result of rising land values the ownership of much of Garden City estate means that it employs 145 people, owns assets to a value of £127m, has an annual income of £7.5m and makes a charitable spend of around £4m. It generates its incomes from property rent, IT Services, a Farm Company, a Cinema and other venues. The monies are spent on community grants, a Day Hospital, Transport services, a Tourist Information Centre, a Museum, Heritage Management and Landscape Management.

The Foundation has this money not so much because of good management of the assets over 110 years, but because they were kept intact as one, so when land values rose because of the town's proximity to London, value of estate rose, this rise was captured for the town, not absent landlords.

There will be those in any city that will argue that nothing more needs to be done, there are no new projects and instead of investing in projects and development it should be refunded as cash to rate payers. This is an old base argument. It will be tempting to pay bonuses to residents, but is a slippery slope. Pay out cash and the city simply becomes a quasi-business and the people, common shareholders and all from the richest to the poorest preferring money in their pocket than a project to help say, the homeless or the mentally ill.

Locking in prosperity with a local currency

What is a local \ alternative \ complimentary currency?

A Community Currency is often used as synonym for complementary currency, local currency, regional currency, alternative currency, auxiliary currencies, and private currencies. All are currencies that have different designs and serve different purposes than conventional money. They depart from the notion that money is essentially a human invention and instrument to influence the relations between citizens and organisations. A solid theoretical framework legitimises this idea and in the past hundred years a lot of experimentation and experience was picked up with realising social goals by the implementation of community currencies.

While the definition of what a local currency is seemed mired in academic debate, its practice isn't and success stories abound. The strength of a local currency is that while it can be complimentary with a national currency it can only be spent locally. In fact, it is usually circulated through local restaurants and shops and as a way to exchange local goods and services. It can't be taken out of the city and so in terms of the Garden City it is a useful instrument for keeping finance and prosperity locked into the city. Not everyone can exchange the money for national currency (some companies, shops and the local tax office).

Local currencies can be issued by different sectors:

- **Private sector**, as with the Swiss Wir that has been operating for over 75 years and is a major source of support for small businesses (see box 31).

- **Public sector**, as with the Bristol Pound. In Bristol the new currency is effectively made real by the local council who have agreed to allow people to pay their local taxes using the currency. In this case, the council can exchange the money for Sterling (see box 29).

- **Community**, as with Palmas Bank in Brazil (see box 30)[30].

But in considering the use of local currencies, it is interesting to consider the whole idea of money and the seminal Wörgl experiment described in box 28 is a useful example. It was conducted from July 1932 to November 1933 is a classic example of the potential efficacy of local currencies. Wörgl, a small town in Austria with 4000 inhabitants, introduced a local script during the Great Depression.

Box 28. The Wörgl experiment

In 1931 the local council of Wörgl in Austria found itself heavily in debt against the background of economic depression and rising unemployment. They had amassed large debts and were unable to provide civic services or continue with local projects. As a solution instead of paying staff wages they issued them labour certificates - Wörgl Bills - to the value of their wages. These certificates became exchangeable for goods and services. They were what is known as a stamp script currency. This meant that they could be converted into cash but only at 98% of face value, also the scripts would automatically depreciate in value by 1% each month unless a special stamp was bought and affixed to it. Because nobody wanted to pay this devaluation (hoarding) fee the Bills were spent as fast as possible, thus improving cash flow in the town.

They proved a great success and effectively refinanced the council allowing them to carry out all their intended works projects and in 23 months allowed them to build new houses, a reservoir, a ski jump, and a bridge. Local government revenue rose from 2,400 AS in 1931 to 20,400 in 1932. Local unemployment was eliminated. No increase in prices was observed. But it met with stiff opposition from the Austrian central bank. As a result, the program was suspended, unemployment rose, and the local economy soon degenerated to the level of other communities in the country.

Box 29. The Bristol Pound

The Bristol Pound[31] is the UK's first city wide local currency, the first to have electronic accounts managed by a regulated financial institution, and the first that can be used to pay some local taxes. Residents can spend Bristol Pounds using paper money, on the internet (using a special account) or through a mobile phone. It is a complimentary currency, designed to work alongside sterling, not replace it. It is not legal tender and so accepting it is voluntary.

Box 30. Banco Palmas, Fortaleza, Brazil

Banco Palmas is a community bank which was founded in 1998 in a 32,000 inhabitants slum called Conjunto Palmeira in Fortaleza, Brazil. It operates under the principle of the "Solidarity Socio-Economy". The "Bank" is managed locally an association of residents and its staff mostly volunteer. Its local alternative currency is called the Palma and is only accepted within the boundaries of the neighbourhood. Converting the Palma into Reals, the official Brazilian currency, can be done at any time at the community bank, but this is discouraged through the imposition of a two per cent administration fee. The Palma circulates side-by-side to the official Brazilian currency and is accepted by local traders, transport providers and even gas stations.

Box 31. WIR and WIR Bank[32]

WIR is a Swiss based cooperative bank that was founded by 16 entrepreneurs in 1934 as a result of the adverse economic and monetary conditions resulting from the Great Depression. It was conceived as a way to stimulate trade and create purchasing power between participants, primarily SMEs, thereby enabling local economic growth and reducing unemployment.

It acts as a "central bank" issuing its own currency – the WIR franc (CHW), which is pegged to the Swiss franc (CHF) and released to members through loans and mortgages backed by collateral. It also acts as a "commercial bank" and has been subject to relevant banking regulations in Switzerland since 1936. It provides a WIR platform through which members can exchange goods and services using the WIR franc as a partial or full means of payment.

Today, about one in five SMEs in Switzerland is a WIR member, resulting in over 60,000 SMEs trading with each other within the WIR system, one third are from the construction industry. It is often seen as a trading mechanism sustaining local economic development and SME growth, especially as SMEs account for 98% of all companies in Switzerland.

Prosperity is shared - Participatory Budgeting

In the earlier chapter on Citizenship we discussed participatory budgeting. The way to move from paternalism and charity to a more active environment is just to spend monies on 'good works' but to give people a say and decision making power in how it is spent. The principle behind this is to say that not only should prosperity be shared, but also a share in the decision making on how it is distributed. It is about moving from the situation where the 'great and the good' decide for everyone else to a situation where everyone gets to decide and participate. There is a clear and unmistakable line between participatory budgeting and participatory democracy; its implementation is a key principle and a major building block of any Garden City

Over the last 20 years, many of the cities in South America have given birth to a number of social movements and the most successful creation of these movements has been a democratic concept of Participatory Budgeting.

At the end of the 1980s, a few cities in Brazil starting applying the principle, organized neighbourhoods joined as decision makers in the processes of allocating municipal budget for public works. 10 years later, there were 100 cities in Latin America applying participatory budgeting and some of them were deciding large percentages of the municipal budgets in participatory assemblies, which is a strong link between budgeting and citizenship. In 2010, 25 years after the first experiences, more than 1500 municipalities around the world followed and adapted the example of the pioneer Brazilian cities, each one applying it in their own way and for different sorts of public spending. Over 150 African cities have been experimenting with it since the early 2000s and more recently China has been introducing it on a massive scale, primarily in Chengdu (see box 32), Chengdu experiment]. The influence has been expanding to some towns in Europe as well. Research is also suggesting that participatory budgeting helps to reduce inequalities, tax evasion and corruption.

Sharing Prosperity - What should happen in practice

- Right to participate in decision making

- Prosperity is not there to generate 'phoney jobs'

- Nor is it there to fund excessive executive pay for employees of the Garden City

- Prosperity needs to be locked into the Garden City so it can't be taken out

- Arrangements in place to stop people from de-mutualising the Garden City or trying to asset strip it.

Box 32. The large-scale participatory budgeting experience in Chengdu, China

---

A scheme of participatory budgeting in Chengdu (14 to 18 million inhabitants), by far the largest PB in China, with over 50,000 projects funded and implemented over the 2009 -2012 period in over 2300 villages and rural communities. Its central argument is that Chengdu PB goes much beyond spatial justice and the reduction of the growing divide between urban and rural development and living conditions. It goes also much beyond a massive and unique improvement of the day-to-day life of millions of villagers.

PB in Chengdu is introducing democratic changes at local level through deliberation and through more power to simple people. Chengdu PB is posited as part of a unique triangle of innovation: (i) Property rights clarification, and increase security of land use rights of villagers; (ii) mechanism to reduce the gap of urban/ rural basic services provision and (iii) Improvement of quality of public services in rural areas through more democratic autonomy to villagers.

Key Conclusions

Sharing prosperity is about building a fair society and a sustainable community, which is the aim of the Garden City. The Garden City may well hold assets together or in trust and these should be used for the benefit of the Garden City. The difficulty is in deciding what it should be used for. The use of participatory budgeting is a key mechanism that can be used to solve this problem.

The other challenge for any City is to retain its wealth. One way to do this is to look at what wealth is. If wealth is money, then why not follow the example of having a local currency for the City. In Venezuela, the oil company there has been turned into a social enterprise such that the profits are reinvested back into the community. This is very much a Garden City principle and has links with the idea of a fair trade dividend and the ideas behind the Co-operative movement.

The fact also that prosperity is being shared and there is a culture that it is shared this enhances citizenship and creates a reason to hold leaders and managers of the town to account. The challenge is that this sharing of prosperity is not purely a paternalistic model but one linked to empowerment and participation.

It is a purpose of a Garden City to reduce inequalities and in part redistribute wealth by sharing the town's prosperity with everyone.

A Garden City principle is that profits should be used to subsidise services and even run additional ones and target deprivation and give people a hand up. Grants should be awarded to give people a hand up but never a hand out. Prosperity should be shared to enable things to happen. One example could be the management of local community assets like a hall. Let people who want to run bands, sewing clubs, discussion group or karate clubs, run such clubs, let the council run the hall and provide the foundations and facilities.

Indeed, why not support disadvantaged communities elsewhere? Why shouldn't Garden Cities twin with each other internationally, or even nationally, and share expertise and resources to improve each other's lives?

[7] All citizens are equal, all citizens are different

All citizens in a Garden City are equal regardless of how long they have lived there or how many generations of their family have. There are no special privileges for anyone. A Garden City provides support and treats with dignity those with mental and physical disabilities, and values each citizen, irrespective of their religious or sexual orientation.

A Garden City is not an exclusive community. People who live in a Garden City are not better than anyone – more fortunate we hope – but not better. The Garden City is an open and inclusive community. The principles and values that define it promote this idea. The idea of 'gated communities' or streets or developments within its boundaries is an anathema. Garden Cities don't preach equality of wealth, or how much people can earn, but there are principles about sharing the prosperity generated by the town and through ethics and fair trade about how this wealth is generated and how it is spent.

But outside of wealth there still exists an invisible class system which may manifest itself, formally or informally. This class system can be about where people come from, who their parents are and how long their family have lived in the city. It provokes the question: Should people who have lived there for a generation have more rights and privileges than those who have just arrived? It is a hard question to answer; there is an idealistic answer and also a pragmatic one. It prompts further questions: Does citizenship need to be earned? If it is not earned does it have any value and do you need to qualify for it?

Another set of questions related to those who have lived in a town, city, street, suburb, parish or village. Are they more entitled if they have lived there a long time? Should they have greater rights? At what point should people be able to share and enjoy the prosperity of the Garden City? Is it at the point they start contributing to it? Or how long should they have to contribute and at what rate?

Box 33. Milton Parc, Montreal and Burlington Vermont CLTs

One of the reasons why the CLTs in Burlington and Montreal both feel that they are successful is that in order to join the CLT\Co-op prospective members are required to undergo up training and preparatory exchanges and meetings to understand what the Co-op and the CLT are about.

These are tough questions. There is indeed an idealistic answer and pragmatic one and the answer lies between the two. We have discussed before the need for people to wish to become citizens of the Garden City (Also see box 33).

What should haunt us is the idea of the creation of some sort of patrician class. Not one necessarily based on wealth or power but the cultural acceptance that as people have lived somewhere for a long time, or because they are an 'old family' they are somehow more important. These are the foundations on which class and division are built.

The aim must be to stop and confront such oligarchies ever taking real power or influence, which is perhaps one of the greatest difficulties.

When any of these networks are created, the result is 'an old boy's network' that runs a city based on privilege. Newcomers are rejected and made to feel like outsiders. It is the challenge for the Garden City and its governance to stop this from happening. The City exists for the benefit of those who live there now; it is not for those who went before. Otherwise, you will end up with a cliquey closed society that is unwelcoming and unfriendly to those outside; a society that thinks it is better than everyone else and jealously guards rather than shares it largesse and liberties.

All citizens are equal, all citizens are different - What should happen in practice

Basically, the governance of the Garden City needs to be representative and robust and ensure that it can't be dominated by one class of people or be exploited for any vested interest. A simple rule that the terms people can spend on any boards be limited to say a maximum of 4 years after which they would need to take a break of at least 2 years. A similar principle exists where participatory budgeting has been implemented where delegates usually serve with a one or two year mandate in order to rotate power and give space to new citizens. Should delegates fail to uphold the Garden City principles they should be recalled.

Key Conclusions

- Unearned privilege undermines citizenship

- A Garden City must be inclusive not exclusive

- A Garden City is not a gated community

- All can contribute and be rewarded

- All are insiders not outsiders or old boy's network

- The assets of the Garden City are to be there in perpetuity for the benefit of all. The city doesn't belong just to those who live and work there now but to future generations too

21st Century Garden Cities of To-morrow

[8] Fair representation and direct democracy

There is a right to participate in the Garden City, in what the city does, how it is run and who does what. A Garden City can be made up of many cities and towns but each of these will be comprised of different neighbourhoods and communities, each with differing needs and aspirations. Each community and neighbourhood should be empowered and encouraged to form its own free and open association, council or forum to represent and engage the views and needs of that local community. The Garden City will share its decision making. It will devolve some to representatives but also by engaging directly and meaningfully with the citizens so all can have an informed say and collective decision making power on the priorities for the Garden City. One example could be participatory budgeting.

The scale of a Garden City could be huge. It doesn't have to be a tiny hamlet, small village or a town the size that Howard specified. In fact, Howard's original vision wasn't of one isolated Garden City but of a network of towns, each with between 30,000 and 50,000 inhabitants [see diagram next page]. The idea was that they would be independent but inter-connected. In England, this network was never achieved even though Welwyn and Letchworth are relatively close to each other. However, Chengdu, China's fourth biggest City with a population of over 14 million people declared a couple of years ago that it intended to generate a Garden City of about one million inhabitants.

A Garden City isn't something that is defined by architectural principles or layout – though these factors can help – but by the other criteria that we are specifying herein.

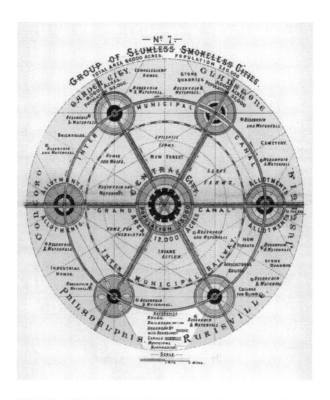

Ebenezer Howard's No.7 diagram of a network of slumless and smokeless cities

A citizen-led city that has built itself on the concepts of fairness and equality will share its wealth and prosperity. But for this to work there is both a need for citizenship and for their citizens to be empowered. By being empowered, they can bring accountability and scrutiny. Without these two virtues, you can end up with a self-serving bureaucracy that simply exists to perpetuate itself and those that control it.

We have discussed the Garden City principles of community ownership and the sharing of wealth and prosperity. Accountability, strong democratic scrutiny and governance underpin all of these.

Governance Models

The fact is that a 'common good' does exist in the garden city and it needs to be derived through negotiation of the key stakeholders in the city. Those are in effect the users, the funders and the workers. In other words, those who live there or nearby whose lives are affected by it, those who work for it and those who fund it. The Burlington model neatly reflects that sort of structure. Burlington as a city isn't entirely a CLT it is a mixed community, the CLT needs to engage with the wider community (See box 34).

Fair Representation

There is a need to ensure strong governance to represent all strands of society. Elections on their own aren't enough. There needs to be democracy between elections which combines fair representation through elections with direct democracy and participation.

Box 34. Comparison of two governance models: Letchworth Garden City Heritage Foundation and Burlington CLT

Letchworth Garden City has a governance model that looks good on paper. The Heritage Foundation that owns most of Letchworth land and manages the benefits of leasing it   combines for its board directly elected representatives with local authority representatives plus general appointed governors plus ones 'appointed' by clubs and societies and the same income group. The clubs and societies do not include tenants or residents associations. There are 30 Governors: 10 nominated by local clubs, 6 directly elected, and 14 general appointed by the Foundation. There are then 9 people on the Board of Management, 7 governors elected by the governors and 2 from the local authority - 1 from the County Council and 1 from the District Council.

While this model is good on paper it was observed in 2009 that most governors tended to live in the same part of town, were drawn from the same clubs and societies. In a town poll that year residents voted in favour of making all the governors and the board democratically elected, Though this recommendation wasn't implemented new leadership at the Foundation has meant that this is starting to improve, But a garden city needs to put its faith not just in good leadership but a strong constitution.

> **Burlington CLT (Champlain Housing Trust)** seems to
> have been more successful in practice in terms of
> governance model. Its Board is made up of a third of
> directors from CLT homeowners, one third from the
> community in Burlington at large (not tenants or
> homeowners in the CLT) and one third from the public
> at large. These public directors tend to be local
> politicians, people in the media or with legitimacy and
> influence locally.

Where there are elections the constituencies that are
represented need to be at a neighbourhood or
community level. If homes are classified by a tax band
as they are in the UK, to ensure equal representation
why not force elections by these bands, or through a
system of representation that would consider the
percentage of people in each of these bands, or
through a system of quotas? There is a need to ensure
strong enough processes are in place to stop any small
unrepresentative group or clique from dominating the
Garden City. The governance of the Garden City
needs to stretch across the whole city to be clear and
its makeup should reflect that of the people who live
there.

A Garden City without strong governance and accountability simply becomes a town run by a landlord.

In order to produce a sustainable community, empowered citizens and harmonious cities, towns, villages and streets then it is necessary to find a glue that binds together houses, streets, factories and offices from being just buildings with people in them to being empowered harmonious communities.

That glue is citizenship and what makes it stick is direct democracy and fair representation. Such that people have control over those people who represent them with a degree of scrutiny and sanction. But this isn't just a democracy of the wealthy or the powerful, nor a situation where a majority can elect to ignore or neglect the poorer minority. Nor is it the situation prevalent in the west in Britain where the middle classes not only recognise the power of action but the power of the ballot box to sustain themselves and their values.

Grassroots Democracy

Democracy and representation need to start at a low level and it will be a task for the higher officials and representatives of the GC to ensure that it works for *all*.

A town is not one simple set of people but of many overlapping communities with differing needs, which may not be purely geographic in nature. For instance, communities may be based on interests, age (young, old, families) or based on wealth – rich and poor – or on ethnicity. Also, many neighbourhoods with differing needs, which will be geographic in nature. For instance, there can be pockets of deprivation in an otherwise prosperous area or prosperous pockets in other deprived areas. Both pockets have their rights.

A Garden City must try to achieve that Holy Grail of participatory and direct democracy. The key fact is that it is not a paternalistic organization but a participatory one. It is not there either just to speak up for or on behalf of people or to do things on their behalf. It is there to empower people, groups, communities and neighbourhoods to make them change themselves. Mass participation may not always be possible and when it is, it is usually only in reaction to something happening that people disagree with, like when a school or a hospital is closing down.

So representation is necessary. In places like Venezuela where street committees and community councils are established, people with a passion, desire and ambition make a change and improve their communities and their lives. The difference is that someone is telling people that 'yes you can' make a difference. It is a powerful message. Instead of negatively complaining and moaning at people it positively empowers and encourages them.

This is the role for the Garden City, to put in place structures and to help and support people do this. For instance, in Letchworth Garden City the former council provided staff whose role it was to help people through the maze of legal, financial and other barriers that can wear down community activists. They sorted out bureaucracy and form filling so that activists could focus on their communities, not on their administration.

The complex legal form filling culture in Britain is more supportive of a middle class environment that is likely to have a solicitor and accountant in its ranks than that of a poorer community. This is the vacuum that the Garden City needs to help fill to empower those other communities.

Key Conclusions

Unless those leading the Garden City can be held to account and their actions fairly scrutinised the Garden City will not work because it could mean that prosperity cannot be fairly shared. There is a risk that privilege can develop and that the Garden City could be exploited by individuals.

A Garden City stands and falls on good governance, good governance is a duty of each citizen. Common ownership suggests common control and this needs to be exercised and put into practice. In the West, there is a disinclination to practice direct and participatory democracy; people are convinced that 4 yearly elections are sufficient.

A successful Garden City has the collective power and strength to be a force for good and to empower communities. However, if this power is placed in the wrong hands then it has the potential to be a repressive and oppressive force.

That is why the governance of the Garden City is so important; it can't be left to chance or done in the hope that the chief executive or leader will be progressive, or to rely on the good will or good nature of the people who will run it.

[9] Garden Cities are produced through participatory planning and design methods

A Garden City is in harmony with the landscape, water, air, nature and the surrounding countryside. New developments and housing have Garden City space and design characteristics, aim to promote the health and wellbeing of its citizens, current and future and are developed through participatory methods on fundamental issues, not just cosmetic ones. Public spaces are widely available as an important concept as it provides the means for people to meet and share views and to integrate. These public spaces and facilities bring together young and old, rich and poor, those of different races, religions and backgrounds as a community that celebrates and rejoices in its diversity and exercises tolerance and freedom.

Libraries have more books on Garden City architecture as the main ingredient for a new town than it does on the actual Garden City social philosophy and its underlying principles and values that make it possible.

When people think about Letchworth and other Garden Cities in England, they have a vision of chocolate box houses and cottages. They assume that there will be lots of flowers planted and green spaces, it will be nice and quaint. Letchworth does provide this image with its arts and craft style of housing, its green walkways and the green feel of the city. There is nothing wrong with that, but that as we have discussed that is not the be-all or end-all of a Garden City.

When looking at Garden City concepts students will also look to some of the larger cities in the world, like Canberra and Stalingrad that were inspired by the Garden City movement. They will also cast an eye over the many new post-war towns in England, such as Letchworth's neighbour, Stevenage, that was also 'inspired' by the Garden City ideal. It is suggested that Garden Cities are the acceptable face of town planning.

The library has more books on Garden City architecture as the main ingredient for a new town than it does on the actual Garden City philosophy, but without people and a sense of community, architecture is just buildings. The original Garden City creed of the three magnets of bringing the best of town and country together is a strong one. It was an ideal from which a technique would develop.

Architecture is important, but it is a means to an end. Good housing, pedestrian areas, green ways, space for growth, space for growing vegetables, green spaces and communal land, all where possible are strong visual characteristics of a Garden City and help to deliver those intangible characteristics too. Yet we state that these are not the only criteria to be a Garden City. The presence of these characteristics helps the others to become a reality. This is because the Garden City is about people and humane values, not buildings.

American author and urbanist Jane Jacobs in 'The Death and Life of Great American Cities' warned several decades ago:

"Cities have the capability of providing something for everybody, only because, and only when, they are created by everybody."

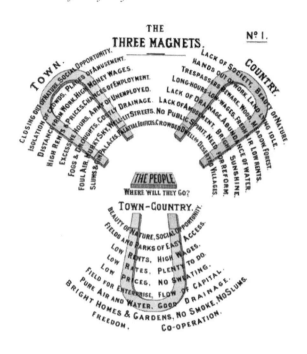

Ebenezer Howard's 3 magnets diagram

A Garden City is an inclusive community, not an exclusive one. A gated community or a high income community, even when it applies garden city design principles cannot claim to be a Garden City. A Garden City is about all strands of society living together in harmony.

Box 35. Benefits of participatory planning and design

Eldonian Village, Liverpool Faced with the threat of their community being broken up and the people being forced to move from their homes in inner-city Liverpool, local people came together in 1978 to keep their community alive and improve the bad housing conditions in the area which they lived. Through tenacity, commitment and much hard work they provided good quality and affordable rental homes, as well as improving the commercial, physical and economic prospects in the area. Twenty-five years later 400 rented houses have been provided, 250 permanent jobs have been provided in business enterprises, $45 million of assets have been created and $180 million of inward investment attracted. The structure of the Eldonian organisation has been specifically designed to ensure control by the local community, to give opportunities for scrutiny and direction and to ensure that local people are ultimately in charge of their future. A board of volunteers drawn from the local residents takes all management decisions.

Box 36. Limits of lack of participatory design in Letchworth Garden City

Jackman's estate.is a public housing development in Letchworth Garden City, but an island in the town ringed off from the rest of it by main roads. In 2003, a survey of residents found that people living there did not consider themselves to be part of the 'Garden City'. They thought of the Garden City as being the older part of town. In this example and its consequences, one can only reflect on how substandard transport links and design failed the Garden City. This seems far from the inclusive society that Ebenezer Howard had hoped for.

Public Spaces

Public spaces are widely available as an important concept to provide the means for people to meet and share views and socialise. These public spaces and facilities bring together young and old, rich and poor, those of different races, religions and backgrounds as a community that celebrates and rejoices in its diversity and exercises tolerance and freedom.

A key principle for generating liveable spaces and adapting garden city principles to citizen's needs and expectations is that these citizens have the right to participate in its design, to change it through time too, to keep up with new necessities and challenges. Garden city architects and planners facilitate this process instead of imposing their views and their vision to future residents.

Without people and a sense of community, architecture is just buildings.

Precedents to the first garden city: early utopians communities

The first Garden City was founded as Letchworth in 1903, but it had been preceded by a number of other new developments that chose to take a new approach to house and community building. Early influences exist such as the work done by Robert Owen with New Lanark and New Harmony in the USA and further back in the British culture was the Diggers Movement, which claimed common land after the civil war. But at the end of the 19th century, a number of industrialists took to looking at the conditions that their workers lived in. These were mainly industrialists from the burgeoning soap and chocolate industries, which result in the new communities of New Earswick, Bournville, Port Sunlight and Saltaire that were a source of inspiration and of reference for envisioning and building the first garden city.

Bournville[33] was built in Birmingham by George Cadbury. It was to be a factory town with a difference. The aim was to build homes of a decent quality at prices within the reach of the industrial workers. It was stated that it was, "...intended to make it easy for working men to own houses with large gardens, secure from the dangers of being spoilt either by factories, or by the interference with the enjoyment of sun, light and air....". In 1893, George Cadbury bought 120 acres (0.5 km²) of land close to the works and began the building of the homes. They were to be for both factory and other local workers.

In 1900, George Cadbury founded Bournville Village Trust, a charitable organisation set up to ensure the planned development and maintenance of the Estate and to preserve it for future generations. In doing so, they moved from building just an estate for workers to live to building a community.

Surplus income was to be used to develop, preserve and extend the estate. By 1904, the 120 acre estate had 143 cottages. Today the Estate covers 1000 acres (4 km²), providing a home for some 25,000 people and includes an exceptionally wide range of housing provision. **Bournville**'s green environment reflects the aim of George Cadbury that one-tenth of the Estate should be "...laid out and used as parks, recreation grounds and open space". Cadbury is quoted as saying "But if each man could have his own house, a large garden to cultivate and healthy surroundings - then, I thought, there will be for them a better opportunity of a happy family life."

Port Sunlight[34] was built between 1889 and 1914. It was a factory town for workers at the Lever Brothers Soap Factory in Cheshire. As a model community on 56 acres, by 1914 it had 800 houses with a population of around 3,500. The facilities for the new village included allotments and public buildings including the Lady Lever Art Gallery, a cottage hospital, schools, a concert hall, open air swimming pool, church, and a temperance hotel.

William Lever claimed that Port Sunlight was an exercise in profit sharing, but rather than share profits directly, he invested them in the village. William Lever said, "It would not do you much good if you send it down your throats in the form of bottles of whisky, bags of sweets, or fat geese at Christmas. On the other hand, if you leave the money with me, I shall use it to provide for you everything that makes life pleasant – nice houses, comfortable homes, and healthy recreation".

Preceding these is **Saltaire,** which was founded in 1851 by Yorkshireman, Sir Titus Salt, who was a leading industrialist in the woollen industry. Sir Titus Salt was a textile mill owner and one of the largest employers in Bradford. Industrial expansion had caused Bradford to grow massively in the first half of the 19th century. Industry also produced high levels of pollution, which caused serious health problems in the local population. Unlike most industrialists, Salt was concerned about this damage to health. In 1848,

Salt became mayor of Bradford and attempted to persuade the council to force local factory owners to take measures against the damage they were causing to local health. The council was unwilling to take action and Salt decided to leave Bradford.

In 1850, he announced plans to build a model industrial community called Saltaire at a nearby beauty spot. Saltaire was built in twenty years. Its textile mill was the largest and most modern in Europe. Measures were taken to reduce noise, dust and dirt from the factory floor. Non-polluting smoke burners were used to protect the air quality in the neighbourhood.

The workers were provided with housing, a park, church, school, hospital, library and a range of shops for the workers. Homes were supplied with fresh water and gas and each had an outside toilet. Public baths and wash-houses were built to ensure good sanitation levels[35]. The mill closed down in 1986. Salt is credited with saying: "The cholera most forcibly teaches us our mutual connection. Nothing shows more powerfully the duty of every man to look after the needs of others".

Joseph Rowntree, also a chocolate entrepreneur, had the village of **New Earswick** built. Between 1902 and 1904, 28 houses were built on a plot of 150 acres near the village of Earswick a few miles north of York. The planner was Barry Parker and the architect was

Raymond Unwin, both of whom would work on the new Garden City in Letchworth. Rowntree said, "I do not want to establish communities bearing the stamp of charity but rather of rightly ordered and self-governing communities".[36]

In many ways from each of these examples, some of the future garden city can be seen. They are all about good housing, the need for allotments and land and health and wellbeing. The introduction of a managing trust is interesting as is the inclusion in the charter for Bournville of investing future profits into the estate. However, the significant difference between these and Letchworth is that the Garden City wasn't built to be a 'model' community or as an exemplar - even though as the first garden city that is what it became. Letchworth wasn't a small community or just houses for a factory. Letchworth wasn't to be about the charity that Lever talked of but the self-governance suggested by Rowntree.

Participatory planning - What should happen in practice

The design of the Garden City needs to move beyond being a utopia envisioned and designed exclusively by philosophers, planners and architects, for it to function and for there to be ownership there needs to be citizen participation in its design, construction and its operation going forward. As Jane Jacobs, said of the original Garden City[37]:

> *"His aim was the creation of self-sufficient small towns, really very nice towns if you were docile and had no plans of your own and did not mind spending your life with others with no plans of their own. As in all Utopias, the right to have plans of any significance belonged only to the planner in charge".*

For the new Garden Cities, this issue needs to be addressed. People need to be involved and have a say in the decision making process, not just consulted. It is not about paternalism, it is about empowerment. There are many ways and numerous examples to do so, one of them being the "Charrette" system for consultations with communities (See box 37).

Box 37. What is a "charrette"?

A "Charrette" combines creative, intense working sessions with public workshops and open houses. It is a collaborative planning process that harnesses the talents and energies of all interested parties to create and support a master plan that represents transformative community change. [38]

Key Conclusions

- Involve people and respect their decision

- Success factor is when people consider it to be their 'town', 'estate', 'home' etc., not the planners

- The design role cannot be left exclusively to the planners. They simply need to facilitate the process bringing with them technical and professional support to help develop the dialogue between people

- Design of public spaces with citizens is crucial

- Use of a Charrette or similar system as a participatory planning process

[10] A City of Rights that builds and defends the Right to the City

In the Garden City, there are universal rights for all citizens such as the right to clean air, the right to nutritious food, the right to adequate housing, the right to work and fair wages. There are not only individual rights but also collective rights, such as the collective right to enjoy the city and its majesty as well as collective civic and political rights. In traditional terms, as the City is held in common there is a collective right to these commons. The Right to the City is a superior Right as it is both individual and collective.

These rights to clean air, housing as well as collective political and civic rights are themselves the outcome of implementing the Garden City principles. But note there a collective right to the City. A right to participate in its envisioning, planning, design and building and a right to enjoy the City and all it has to offer. It is about inclusivity that the City is there for everyone. That everyone has the right to participate in its design, developing its vision and its implementation. The City and the people in it have these collective rights; they are not just individual rights but collective ones too

> *The right to the city is far more than the individual liberty to access urban resources: it is a right to change ourselves by changing the city. It is, moreover, a common rather than an individual right since this transformation inevitably depends upon the exercise of a collective power to reshape the processes of urbanisation. The freedom to make and remake our cities and ourselves is, I want to argue, one of the most precious yet most neglected of our human rights*
> *(David Harvey)[39]*

Like the common land that once existed in England, there was a right to use these 'commons'. The Garden City is no different, it too is held in common and people have a collective right to it.

[11] Knowledge is held in common, shared and enhanced

A Garden City is a mutual city that builds a culture of production, sharing and co-operation, not just in terms of its prosperity and governance, but also in terms of the knowledge it acquires and generates. It shares and co-operates for the good of the City while still operating competition to create innovation and development.

The Garden City is about co-operation and innovation. It shares its knowledge for the development of the City and the benefit of all. If the prosperity of the city has invested in and helped develop this new knowledge then the City itself can claim a moral investment and dividend from it.

For instance, in Cuba there is a huge focus on urban agriculture. The success from the project has come from people, neighbourhoods and cities throughout the island sharing new techniques and ideas and as a consequence, the City has flourished as the world leader in urban agriculture. It is a great example of development and growth through mutual co-operation. What is important is that it is not just knowledge that has been shared but 'know-how' too on how to live better in a city and contribute to its building as a unique and collective masterpiece.

Knowledge should not only be shared among local citizens but with other citizens in the world. Sharing knowledge with other cities will contribute to transforming people and their cities into Garden Cities. It will improve at the same time knowledge, know-how and visions of those living in the Garden city. Sharing knowledge is a two-way transformative process.

[12] Wealth and harmony measured by happiness

The wealth and harmony of the Garden City is measured through the happiness of its citizens. It is the only true measurement of a successful city. Their happiness is not based upon the suffering or expense of others.

"It is like being in love, no one can tell you that you are in love, or force you to be in love, you just know it." [40]

How do you measure the success of a Garden City? Obviously, you can't measure it only in its prosperity and material wealth. A barrio in Caracas can be a Garden City just as a suburb of Manhattan can be. The measure of success needs to be measured from the harmony, health and happiness of its citizens.

A Garden City on its own cannot generate wealth but it can create the conditions in which prosperity can flourish. A Garden City seeks to create harmony between town and country and between citizens and those that represents them and govern them.

Box 38. The International Day of Happiness? [41]

On 20 March 2013, the first ever International Day of Happiness was celebrated worldwide. The day was proclaimed by the UN General Assembly to promote happiness as a universal goal and aspiration in the lives of people around the globe.

The initiative to declare a day of happiness came from the Kingdom of Bhutan – a country whose Gross National Happiness Index takes the view that sustainable development should take a holistic approach towards progress and give equal importance to non-economic aspects of wellbeing.

The International Day of Happiness recognises the efforts of other nations and groups who work to measure prosperity that go beyond material wealth.

By designating a special day for happiness, the UN aims to focus world attention on the idea that economic growth must be inclusive, equitable, and balanced, such that it promotes sustainable development and eliminate poverty.

An objective of the New Garden City Movement is to try to define ways of measuring health, wealth, happiness and harmony but by its very nature, what is to be measured is intangible and defies attempts at measurement. It is like being in love, no one can tell you that you are in love, you just know.

Conclusion

A Garden City is a town that brings together the best elements of town and country. Its aim is to be economically, socially and environmentally sustainable and it will underwrite these goals by adopting the 12 social GC principles as its constitution.

This will ensure that the rising value of the land in the town will be captured in perpetuity for the good of the community. Meaning that the town will always be able to provide affordable homes and own the resources to ensure its long-term economic viability.

This requires that the majority of the land is owned by a community trust that is democratically administered by the community so that its prosperity is shared and retained within the town.

These elements will combine together to create citizens of the Garden City who have a sense of place and belonging, as it will be tangibly underwritten through real community ownership and active participation in it.

The twelve principles that we have outlined are the key principles upon which any Garden City should be built. In short, what we are saying is that if you want to build or become a garden city then you should take these twelve principles and apply them.

There are two ways of looking at the principles, the first is to see them as painting a picture of a garden city, and the second is to see them as both entries and exits to and from the garden city philosophy.

Like any portrait, the brush strokes are what are important. Some will be more defined than others will and so it may be true of the garden city principles. It may be easier to apply some rather than others, and some of them may be hard to apply at all, in which you will need to compensate with the ones you have used. The end result will be that when looking at it in its entirety it will look like a Garden City.

The alternative way is to see the principles as both entries and exits to the Garden City. Adoption of any of the principles allows for entry into the Garden City house, but refusal to adopt a principle will also make it an exit. Some principles may be easier to put into practise than others may and there will always be different ways to view this. For instance, if a developer rejects the idea of community land ownership, then this is an exit for them. However, if a group can't get community ownership of the land, only use of it, then this isn't necessarily an exit.

So, while we do see the principles as being embraced by developers of new settlements, both for suburbs and towns, we also see them as being applicable to existing towns and communities. Existing communities should have the power to adopt the principles through social campaigning and action and have the ability to adopt the 'garden city' suffix for their communities. One of key messages after all is that the Garden City is about social values not architecture. The Garden City is not built on charity and paternalism but on citizenship and empowerment.

As for the principles themselves, we see them as being the ethical base needed to achieve sustainability in three key areas. These are environmental sustainability, economic sustainability and social sustainability. These are inter-connected but can be achieved through the adoption of the twelve principles. Environmental and ethical sustainability is achieved through land sharing, shared heating, urban agriculture and fair trade as described earlier. Economic sustainability is achieved through the endowment of land to the community (through a CLT or a CLB). Thirdly, the Garden City should deliver social sustainability, which is around affordability. This again links with the common and perpetual ownership of the land. The Garden City cannot become a gated community or home for the rich, it needs to sustain affordability in the city to accommodate all peoples. The examples given earlier in the text of Chicago and in Burlington to sustain affordability through their CLT structure remain as strong examples. Binding and holding these objectives together are the twelve principles and they need to be maintained through strong, democratic and accountable community governance. The twelve principles can be the mechanism or agenda for implementing the long-term governance of the city.

So if you want to build or create a Garden City, what do you need to do? The answer is to adopt the twelve principles as horizons and as practical ways to approach it.

We are not asking the impossible and neither are we suggesting anything unrealistically utopian. For all the principles are based on real examples and past practise. All the methods work on their own though the goal of the Garden City is to bring them together to magnify their effects and benefits.

In practise, you should define a 'constitution' for your garden city. Within this constitution should be the twelve principles as your goals. You should turn these goals into a long-term strategic plan, from which you should formulate the projects to implement the goals. For each project, you and the inhabitants should define key performance indicators to measure progress and success. This constitution should form part of the master plan for the settlement and form the agenda that scrutinise and gives a base to the governance of the new garden city, whether for a new council or a community owned company that would manage the estate.

You do not have to do this alone, there are many in the garden city movement willing and able to help. We ask that you always remember that the Garden City is not just an architectural or an urban planning project but is a social project. The ultimate goal is what is written as the 12th and final principle - 'Wealth and harmony measured by happiness'. It is a straightforward and an unambiguous goal. It may not sound like a defining social and political goal. But it doesn't need to be. As people, we want to see a happy and harmonious society for our brothers, sisters and all the people we care for. Perhaps no single goal can be as simple or as great.

Further Reading

Benn, T. (2011) *Gerrard Winstanley - A Common Treasury*, Versobooks.

Cabannes, Y. (2004) Participatory Governance, in *Participatory Governance*, Vol. 16, No. 1, April.

Cabannes, Y. (2004) 72 Frequently Asked Questions about Participatory Budgeting, UN-Habitat publications. Available at: http://www.unhabitat.org/documents/faqqPP.pdf [Accessed Dec 2013]

Cancela, J. (2009) Urban Agriculture in City Planning Process: Experiences from Portugal, *45th ISOCARP Congress*, available at: http://www.isocarp.net/Data/case_studies/1402.pdf. [Accessed December 2013]

Conaty, P. and Large, M. (2013) *Common Sense - Cooperative place making and the capturing of land value for 21st century Garden Cities*, Co-operatives UK Limited. Available: http://www.uk.coop/sites/storage/public/downloads/commons_sense.pdf [Accessed 2013]

Danish Architecture Centre. (n.d.) Havana feeding the city on urban agriculture, [online], available: http://www.dac.dk/en/dac-cities/sustainable-cities-2/all-cases/food/havana-feeding-the-city-on-urban-agriculture/?bbredirect=true [Accessed December 2013]

Dickens, C. (n.d.). A Christmas Carol.

Hackney, R (1990) *The Good, the Bad and the Ugly: Cities in Crisis*, Frederick Muller Ltd.

Harvey, D. (2008) The Right to the City, in *New Left Review,* Vol. 53, pp. 23-40.

Howard, E. (1902) *Garden Cities of To-morrow*. London: S. Sonnenschein & Co. Ltd.

Kang, V. (2011) *An effectiveness comparison between two different affordable housing provision approaches, Inclusionary Housing and Community Land Trust, through the cases of England. Which should be given a priority of public support?*, MSc Thesis, International Institute of Urban Management, Rotterdam, The Netherlands. Available: http://oaithesis.eur.nl/ir/repub/asset/11558/(1)35646.pdf [Accessed Dec 2013].

Jacobs, J. (1961) *The Death and Life of Great American Cities*, New York: Random House.

Lewis, M. and Conaty, P. (2012) The Resilience Imperative: Cooperative Transitions to a Steady-state Economy, New Society Publishers. Available: http://www.newsociety.com/Books/R/The-Resilience-Imperative [Accessed Dec 2013]

Lewis, M. & Turnball, S. (2011) The Co-operative Land Bank : A Solution in Search of a Home, available: http://communityrenewal.ca/sites/all/files/resource/i42011NOV30_Landbanks.pdf [Accessed Dec 2013].

Livingstone, G. (2010) *America's Bankyard*, London: ZED Books.

Ross, P. (2011) New Garden City Movement, in Chang, M and L. Meusburger (eds), *The Food Junctions Cookbook: Living Recipes for Social Innovation*, London: UCL London.

UN-Habitat (n.d.) Green Mortgages, available: http://www.worldhabitatawards.org/winners-and-finalists/project-details.cfm?lang=00&theProjectID=9DA03455-15C5-F4C0-99170E7D631F50E9. [Accessed Dec 2013]

Web sites

Champlain Housing Trust (Burlington)

http://www.champlainhousingtrust.org/

http://www.burlingtonassociates.com

CLT Network (UK)

http://www.communitylandtrusts.org.uk/home

CLT Network (USA)

http://www.cltnetwork.org

Fair Trade Foundation (UK)

http://www.fairtrade.org.uk/

Letchworth Garden City Heritage Foundation

http://www.letchworthgc.com

Letchworth Citizens Forum

http://lgcforum.blogspot.co.uk/

Locality (UK)

http://locality.org.uk

Housing Assistance Council (USA)

http://216.92.48.246/pubs/CLT/contents.htm

Masdar City

http://masdarcity.ae/en/

Milton Park Community, Montreal

http://www.miltonparc.org/en/

Owenstown

http://www.owenstown.org/index.php

SCOPS (France)

http://www.les-scop-idf.coop/

Town and Country Planning Association (TCPA - UK)

http://www.tcpa.org.uk/

Transitions Town Movement

http://www.transitionnetwork.org/

Index

End Note

[1] The Arts and Crafts Movement began in Britain around 1880 and quickly spread to America, Europe and Japan. Inspired by the ideas of John Ruskin and William Morris, it advocated a revival of traditional handicrafts, a return to a simpler way of life and an improvement in the design of ordinary domestic objects.

The Movement took its name from the Arts and Crafts Exhibition Society, founded in 1887, but it encompassed a very wide range of like-minded societies, workshops and manufacturers. Other countries adapted Arts and Crafts philosophies according to their own needs. While the work may be visually very different, it is united by the ideals that lie behind it (source - http://www.vam.ac.uk/page/a/arts-and-crafts/)

[2] The Welfare State of Britain was the result of the William Beveridge Report in 1942, which identified five 'Giant Evils' in society: squalor, ignorance, want, idleness and disease.

[3] CLTs in Montreal, Canada and Vermont in the USA

[4] *Housing and Regeneration Act 2008*, Part 2, Chapter 1, Section 79

[5] www.parliament.uk/briefing-papers/SN04903.pdf

[6] http://communityrenewal.ca/co-op-landbanks

[7] Highland Park Community Land Trust in Illinois, USA
http://www.hpiclt.org/about-us

[8] Diacon, D., Clarke, R. and Guimarães, S. (Eds) (2005) *Redefining the Commons Locking in Value through Community Land Trusts*, Joseph Rowntree Foundation , Coalville: Building and Social Housing Foundation.

[9] The model in the UK is slightly different

[10] Co-operative Land Banks – a modern model to capture wealth for new Garden Cities by Shann Turnbull, International Institute for Self-governance. Taken from Common-Sense. Edited by Pat Conaty, Co-operatives UK and Martin Large, Stroud Common Wealth - published 2013

[11] http://www.sacred-texts.com/utopia/gcot/gcot04.htm

[12] Lewis and Turnbull - Nov 2011 http://www.scribd.com/doc/148388734/The-Co-operative-Land-Bank

[13] Called the Scheme of Management, residents have no independent right of appeal against any decision other than in the past to take it to the High Court.

[14] https://www.duedil.com/company/IP28211R/letchworth-garden-city-heritage-foundation and local leaflets

[15] Common Sense - Edited by Pat Conaty, Co-operatives UK and Martin Large, Stroud Common Wealth - December 2013

[16] An environmentally friendly city

[17] Masdar city : http://masdarcity.ae/en/

[18] Transition Towns definition http://www.farmgarden.org.uk/transition-towns-movement

[19] Taken from Wikipedia

[20] FUCVAM - http://www.worldhabitatawards.org/winners-and-finalists/project-details.cfm?
lang=00&TheProjectID=9DC73800-15C5-
F4C0-99F350F027EC172E

[21] What is Urban Agriculture? - RUAF - http://www.ruaf.org/node/512

22 History of UK Allotments - http://www.allotment.org.uk/articles/Allotment-History.php

23 Havana Cuba - Urban Agriculture - http://www.dac.dk/en/dac-cities/sustainable-cities/all-cases/food/havana-feeding-the-city-on-urban-agriculture/?bbredirect=true

24 By Philip Ross, council newsletter

25 Programme for Endorsement of Forest Certification (PEFC) - http://www.pefc.org/about-pefc/who-we-are

26 Authors note : Don't confuse these with taxes, those will still be charged by the municipality. This is revenue\dividend from the town's assets and services that are collectively owned

27 Winstanley said: This earth divided, we will make whole. So it can be a common treasury for all.

28 72 Frequently Asked Questions on Participatory Budgeting http://www.unhabitat.org/documents/faqqPP.pdf

29 Co-operative Movement http://www.gdm32.dial.pipex.com/about%20the%20co-operative%20movement.htm

30 Palmas Bank - Notes http://casepalmas.files.wordpress.com/2012/10/case-palmas-pdf.pdf

31 The Bristol Pound - http://bristolpound.org

32 Sources: http://en.wikipedia.org/wiki/WIR_Bank and http://www.lfig.org/articles/new-cooperative-banking-model-empowering-communities-swiss-style/

33 Bournville Village Trust - https://www.bvt.org.uk/

34 Port Sunlight - http://www.portsunlightvillage.com/

35 Taken from: Sir Titus Salt, Baronet: His Life and its Lessons by Robert Balgarnie published by Hodder & Stoughton in 1877

36 New Earswick - http://www.jrht.org.uk/node/26

37 Jane Jacobs discussing Ebenezer Howards' Garden City, in Jacobs, J. (1961) The Death and Life of Great American Cities, pp. 27. New York: Random House.

38 Use of Charrettes for planning and consultation http://www.sandiego.gov/redevelopment-agency/pdf/gvchardesc081110.pdf -

39 The Right to the City - David Harvey, New Left Review 53, September 2008 - http://newleftreview.org/II/53/david-harvey-the-right-to-the-city

40 The Matrix (1999) Film. Paraphrases what the Oracle told Neo about being the One. http://www.imdb.com/title/tt0133093/quotes

41 International Day of Happiness http://www.un.org/en/development/desa/news/social/intl-day-happiness.html